RECOVERY
WITHOUT ROCK BOTTOM

Reclaim Your Life from Addictive Behaviors

ANDREA SEYDEL

Copyright © 2024 by Andrea Seydel

All rights reserved.

Published and Distributed in Canada by Live Life Happy Publishing. www.livelifehappypublishing.com

All rights reserved. No part of this book may be reproduced by any mechanical, photographic, or electronic process, or in the form of a phonograph recording: Nor may it be stored in a retrieval system, transmitted, or otherwise be copied for public or private use- other than for "fair use" as brief quotations embodied in articles and reviews without prior written permission of the publisher. If you use any of the information in this book for yourself, which is your constitutional right, the author and the publisher assumes no responsibility for your actions.

Library of Congress Cataloging-in-Publication Data

Andrea Seydel

Recovery Without Rock Bottom: Reclaim Your Life from Addictive Behaviors

Categories: Self-Help > Substance Abuse & Addictions > Alcoholism Health, Fitness & Dieting > Mental Health > Addiction & Recovery Nonfiction > Social Science > Psychology > Psychotherapy > Counseling

ISBN: 978-1-990461-97-2 Papberback

ISBN: 978-1-990461-98-9 E-BOOK

ISBN: 978-1-990461-99-6 Audio

Cover Design: Andrea Seydel

Live Life Happy Publishing

PUBLISHER'S NOTE & AUTHOR DISCLAIMER

This publication is designed to provide accurate and authoritative information concerning the subject matter covered. It is sold to understand that the publisher and author are not engaging in or rendering any psychological, medical or other professional services. If expert assistance or counselling is needed, seek the services of a competent medical professional. For immediate support call your local crisis line. The following book could contain actual events and experiences that the author has encountered in their life. However, some names and specific locations have been changed or omitted to protect the privacy and confidentiality of the individuals involved. The changes do not alter the story's integrity or its messages.

Dedication

To those who believe in the power of transformation, this is for you. To everyone daring to reclaim their lives, their joy, and their sense of purpose—you are the embodiment of resilience and courage. Recovery isn't about hitting rock bottom; it's about rising into the life you were meant to live. To the loved ones who stand steadfast in the face of uncertainty—I understand YOU. Thank you for your courage, love, and unwavering belief in the possibility of change. To the seekers, the learners, and the everyday heroes who inspire others simply by choosing growth—may this book be your companion, your guide, and your reminder that healing and hope ripple outward in powerful ways. Here's to redefining what it means to recover, rediscovering the beauty in engaging fully in your life, and reclaiming the life you deserve.

With boundless gratitude and hope,

Andrea

Contents

Introduction: A Positive Path of Recovery and Growth 7

PART 1: SHINING A LIGHT ON RECOVERY

Chapter 1: Breaking the Cycle: Illuminating Addictive Behaviors and the Path Forward 13

Chapter 2: Redefining Recovery: Harnessing Well-Being for Lasting Change 25

The RECOVERY Sunshine Assessment: Illuminate Your Path to Well-Being 38

PART 2: THE RECOVERY PRINCIPLES

Chapter 3: Resilience and Growth 47

Chapter 4: Empathy and Self-Compassion 89

Chapter 5: Connection and Positive Relationships 119

Chapter 6: Optimism and Gratitude 153

Chapter 7: Vitality and Health 189

Chapter 8: Engagement and Purpose 221

Chapter 9: Reflection and Mindfulness 255

Chapter 10: You-Focused Empowerment 293

PART 3: BRINGING RECOVERY TO LIFE

Chapter 11: Building Your Recovery Blueprint: Illuminating the Path Forward 335

Chapter 12: Building Lasting Change —From Intentions to Habits 355

Conclusion 369

Introduction: A Positive Path of Recovery and Growth

Introduction to *Recovery Without Rock Bottom*

What comes to mind when you hear the word recovery? Is it addiction treatment centers? 12-step programs? Rock bottom? Maybe you picture someone at their lowest point—broken, desperate, and out of options. That's the image we've been fed for years.

But here's the truth: that image is wrong. We've lost the true meaning of recovery.

Why does recovery have to mean crisis? Why do we tell people to wait until everything falls apart before they can take back their lives? Why does recovery have to feel like a punishment, a label, or a last resort?

Recovery doesn't have to be about hitting rock bottom. In fact, it shouldn't be. Recovery should be about catching yourself before you fall—about rediscovering your purpose, reclaiming your joy, and taking back your life *before* things spiral out of control.

This isn't just an ideal—it's backed by science. Positive psychology, neuroscience, and the science of well-being offer us an entirely new way to think about recovery. It's not about avoiding what's bad; it's about creating a life so good that destructive habits simply don't fit. Recovery isn't just about surviving—it's about thriving.

For too long, traditional recovery models have focused on the extremes—on severe addiction and crisis intervention. While these models are vital for those at the edge, they leave out so many people.

What about the "in-betweeners"?

The in-betweeners are the people who know their habits aren't serving them but don't see themselves as addicts. Maybe it's the nightly bottle of wine that's turned into two, or the endless social media scroll that's draining hours from their day. These behaviors may not yet be catastrophic, but they're taking up space in their lives—space that could be filled with joy, purpose, and connection.

And what do these people think? "I'm not bad enough to need help." Or worse, "I don't have a problem. Recovery is for people who *really* need it."

This mentality is toxic. It creates denial and discourages action. Why are we waiting for people to hit rock bottom before we help them grow?

This book is for the in-betweeners. It's for the people who don't fit into traditional recovery programs but know something's off. It's for those who are ready to pivot, to grow, and to take back their lives. Recovery doesn't have to mean quitting forever, embracing sobriety, or taking on a label that doesn't resonate.

Recovery is prevention. It's about recognizing the signs early, steering clear of the dangers, and building a life so full of meaning, joy, and connection that unhealthy habits have no room to thrive.

True recovery, in its purest form, is about rediscovery. It's about reconnecting with the person you are at your core—someone who may have been overshadowed by unhelpful habits or patterns. Recovery is about healing, restoring, and reclaiming your innate strength and values.

And here's the best part: change is always possible. Thanks to neuroplasticity, we know that even the most ingrained behaviors and thought patterns can be rewired. Recovery is about creating new pathways and stepping into a life that feels aligned with your purpose and joy.

This book offers a proactive, science-backed approach to recovery. It introduces the RECOVERY Principles—a framework grounded in research and designed to guide you toward a thriving, flourishing life. Each principle serves as a pillar, keeping you steady and empowered.

You'll also discover practical tools to bring these principles to life—like purpose-driven goals, waypower and willpower, implementation intentions, habit formation, and Minimum Viable Interventions. These aren't just ideas—they're actionable steps to help you create real, lasting change.

Recovery isn't about fixing what's broken—it's about reclaiming what's already within you. It's about creating a life so rich with joy, purpose, and connection that there's no room for anything else.

Recovery Without Rock Bottom isn't just a book—it's a movement. It's for anyone who wants to stop waiting for crisis and start building the life they deserve. Recovery is for everyone. And it starts now. Are you ready for recovery?

PART 1

SHINING A LIGHT ON RECOVERY

*"You are not your struggles.
You are the place where change begins."*

– Viktor Frankl

CHAPTER 1

Breaking the Cycle: Illuminating Addictive Behaviors and the Path Forward

To truly understand a behavior is to shine light on it without judgment, to approach it with curiosity instead of shame. Addictive behaviors often arise as pathways we take to avoid pain or seek comfort, yet they can keep us from the fullness of life we desire. When we look at these behaviors with a hopeful perspective, we realize they are not fixed; they are learned, and what is learned can be unlearned. This chapter invites you to see your journey as one of growth, resilience, and possibility—a chance to understand not just where you've been but where you are capable of going.

BREAKING THE CYCLE

"You can't go back and change the beginning, but you can start where you are and change the ending."

– C.S. Lewis

To truly understand a behavior is to shine light on it—not with judgment, but with curiosity and compassion. Addictive behaviors often begin as small, seemingly harmless ways to soothe pain or seek comfort. Yet over time, these patterns can take root and grow, quietly disrupting your sense of balance, joy, and connection to what truly matters.

The hopeful truth is this: **you are not broken, and you are not powerless.** Addictive behaviors are learned, and what is learned can be unlearned. Your brain is capable of healing, adapting, and creating new, healthier patterns. The fact that you're here, reading these words, is proof of your readiness to take a step forward.

This chapter will help you understand where addictive behaviors come from, how they take hold, and—most importantly—how you can break free. It's not about blame or shame. It's about awareness, self-compassion, and the power to reclaim your life.

Seeking Pleasure, Avoiding Pain: How Addictive Behaviors Take Root

At its core, your brain is wired for survival. It has one simple mission: to seek pleasure and avoid pain. This mechanism, designed to keep you safe and thriving, rewards behaviors that bring relief, comfort, or satisfaction.

When you eat food, your brain releases dopamine to motivate you to keep eating and survive.

When you connect with loved ones, the same system rewards you for social bonding.

When you accomplish a goal, dopamine reinforces your efforts, motivating you to strive further.

But addictive behaviors hijack this system. They offer a quick hit of pleasure or relief, releasing an intense flood of dopamine that temporarily feels satisfying. Over time, your brain begins to associate the behavior—drinking, scrolling, binge-eating, using substances—with safety, relief, or happiness.

The tricky part? The reward fades. Your brain adapts, requiring **more of the behavior to feel the same effect**—this is called *tolerance*. What started as a glass of wine becomes a bottle, or what began as a quick scroll becomes hours of distraction. Your brain starts prioritizing the behavior, and before you realize it, it feels less like a choice and more like a need.

This is the **slippery slope**: the gradual progression from a manageable habit to something that feels entrenched, automatic, and hard to break.

The Role of Denial: Why It's So Hard to See the Problem

One of the most powerful barriers to breaking free from addictive behaviors is denial. Denial is sneaky—it minimizes, rationalizes, and avoids the truth to shield you from discomfort. It's not weakness; it's a defense mechanism that helps you avoid facing the deeper impact of the behavior.

Denial often sounds like this:

- *"It's not that bad."* You compare yourself to others who "have it worse" to convince yourself it's not a problem.
- *"I can stop anytime."* Even when attempts to cut back have failed, you hold onto the illusion of control.
- *"Everyone does this."* You normalize the habit because others do it, ignoring how it impacts you personally.
- *"I deserve this."* You justify the behavior as a reward for stress, pain, or hard work.
- *"I'm still functioning."* You believe that as long as you're keeping up with work or obligations, it's not an issue.

Because addictive behaviors often start small and escalate slowly, it's easy to overlook their impact. You may still show up for work, maintain relationships, and appear "fine" on the outside, but underneath, the behavior chips away at your time, energy, and sense of self.

Recognizing denial isn't about judgment—it's about honesty. When you notice these thoughts and question them, you take a critical first step toward clarity, freedom, and change.

Common Addictive Behaviors

Addictive behaviors aren't always obvious. They can appear harmless, even normal, at first. Here are some of the most common ones:

1. **Alcohol**: Increasing reliance on drinks to unwind, relax, or cope.

2. **Social Media**: Endless scrolling that distracts from relationships, work, or rest.

3. **Overeating**: Using food for emotional comfort, leading to cycles of bingeing and regret.

4. **Shopping**: Compulsive buying to feel better, despite mounting debt or clutter.

5. **Substance Use**: Misuse of drugs (recreational or prescription) for escape or relief.

6. **Binge-Watching**: Escaping into TV or videos at the cost of sleep, productivity, or connection.

7. **Pornography**: Excessive use that impacts intimacy, self-esteem, or relationships.

8. **Gaming**: Gaming that becomes all-consuming, replacing meaningful activities.

9. **Nicotine/Vaping**: Dependency on substances to calm anxiety or increase focus.

10. **Workaholism**: Overworking to avoid personal emotions or issues, leading to burnout.

These behaviors may not seem extreme at first, but over time, they can take a significant toll on your health, relationships, and sense of fulfillment.

The Slippery Slope: When Addictive Behaviors Become a Problem

Here's how addictive behaviors quietly take hold:

1. **Relief**: The behavior begins as a way to cope with stress, boredom, or discomfort.

2. **Repetition**: You repeat it because it works—at least temporarily.

3. **Tolerance**: Over time, you need more of it to feel the same relief or satisfaction.

4. **Dependence**: The behavior feels automatic, as if it's no longer a choice.

The slide is subtle, which is why it's so easy to miss. You might think, *"It's not that bad,"* or, *"I'm still in control,"* even as you start to feel drained, disconnected, or stuck.

But here's the hopeful truth: recognizing this progression gives you the power to stop it. You don't have to wait for rock bottom to take back control.

The First Step: Awareness

Awareness is the foundation of change. It's about taking an honest look at your behaviors and asking:

- *How is this habit serving me—or holding me back?*
- *How much time, energy, or focus is this taking from my life?*
- *What would my life look like if I didn't rely on this behavior?*

This process isn't about shame or self-criticism. It's about curiosity—gently noticing the patterns that no longer serve you and opening the door to something better.

The Great News: You Can Break Free

Your brain's neuroplasticity—its ability to rewire itself—means that change is always possible. Just as addictive behaviors were learned, they can be unlearned. With awareness, intentional action, and self-compassion, you can:

- **Break Old Patterns**: The pathways that reinforce harmful habits can fade with disuse.

- **Build New Habits**: Healthier behaviors can replace the old ones through practice and repetition.

- **Reconnect to Joy and Purpose**: By letting go of what no longer serves you, you create space for what truly matters.

Recovery doesn't require rock bottom—it begins with a simple choice: to take one small step forward. No matter where you are, this journey is about progress, not perfection.

Let this be the moment you remind yourself:

I have the power to change.
I can take back my life.
This is just the beginning.

Final Summary

Addictive behaviors may feel overwhelming, but they are not permanent. They are learned responses to life's challenges, and through awareness and intentional effort, they can be unlearned. By understanding how these patterns take hold in your brain and recognizing the signs of dependence, you can begin to reclaim control.

Recovery is not about perfection—it's about progress. Each small step you take toward healthier habits strengthens your brain's ability to adapt and thrive. Through self-compassion, awareness, and action, you can move beyond addictive behaviors and build a life rooted in resilience, connection, and joy.

Key Takeaways

Awareness Is the First Step
Recognizing addictive behaviors and their impact on your life is the foundation of change. Honest self-reflection, without judgment, opens the door to transformation.

Your Brain Can Rewire Itself
Thanks to neuroplasticity, your brain is capable of unlearning harmful patterns and creating new, healthier ones. Each intentional choice reinforces these positive changes.

Recovery Is About Reclaiming Yourself
Recovery isn't just about breaking free from harmful patterns; it's about rediscovering your strengths, building meaningful connections, and creating a life that aligns with your values and goals.

This journey is yours to shape. Each step forward brings you closer to the freedom and fulfillment you deserve. Let this chapter be the beginning of your transformation.

A SPARK of HOPE

If you have addictive behaviors, you are not broken. The patterns you've fallen into were learned, and what is learned can be unlearned. The fact that you're here, reading these words, means that some part of you is ready for change, for growth, for freedom. That readiness is powerful—it's the spark that can light the way forward.

When the road feels difficult or uncertain, remind yourself: you are not your mistakes, nor are you defined by your past. You are capable of growth, of resilience, and of creating a life that reflects your truest self.

What sparked your curiosity or caught your attention?
(Reflect on what you found interesting or intriguing.)

_____
_____
_____
_____
_____

What insights or ideas feel actionable or relevant to your life?
(Identify what you can apply or implement.)

_____
_____
_____
_____
_____

What resonated deeply or felt personally meaningful to you?
(Consider what moved or inspired you emotionally or intellectually.)

_____
_____
_____
_____
_____

CHAPTER 2

Redefining Recovery: Harnessing Well-Being for Lasting Change

What if recovery is not about erasing every challenge, but about learning to rise and thrive alongside them? By embracing the science of human flourishing, we uncover a powerful truth: we are capable of more than survival—we can build lives of deep meaning, connection, and purpose. This chapter invites you to shift your focus from avoiding what pulls you down to actively creating what lifts you up. Through resilience, well-being, and intentional action, you'll discover that recovery is not about what you lose, but about everything you stand to gain.

REDEFINING RECOVERY

"Happiness is not the absence of problems; it's the ability to deal with them." — Martin Seligman

For decades, psychology has been dedicated to studying what's wrong with people—what causes suffering, dysfunction, and disorder. But what if we could study the opposite? What if we could ask, "What makes life worth living? What helps people not just survive, but truly thrive?"

This question sparked a revolutionary movement in the field of psychology—one that led to the study of human flourishing, happiness, and well-being. Led by pioneers like Dr. Martin Seligman, Dr. Mihaly Csikszentmihalyi, and a growing body of well-being researchers, this science focuses on what's *right* with us: our strengths, resilience, and innate potential to live fulfilling, joyful lives—even in the face of challenges.

At the same time, the fields of **neuroscience, behavioral science**, and evidence-based therapies like **Cognitive Behavioral Therapy (CBT)** and **Acceptance and Commitment Therapy (ACT)** have provided powerful tools for understanding how our brains, thoughts, and actions shape our habits and experiences.

As you journey through this book, you'll learn from incredible researchers and pioneers in their fields—names like Martin Seligman, who laid the foundation for positive psychology; Barbara Fredrickson, whose work on positivity ratios reshaped how we view emotions; Tal Ben-Shahar, a champion of practical happiness studies; and Ellen Langer, who brought mindfulness into the mainstream. Each principle in this book is enriched by their groundbreaking discoveries, offering you actionable insights rooted in science.

These disciplines and researchers reveal a hopeful truth: **Change is possible. Healing is possible. Thriving is possible.**

When we bring together the best of these worlds—neuroscience, positive psychology, behavioral science, happiness studies, and evidence-based therapies—we gain a new lens for recovery. One that is not rooted in punishment, labels, or deprivation, but in growth, purpose, and the discovery of what makes life good.

Why Redefine Recovery?

For too long, recovery has been defined as simply breaking free from harmful behaviors or addictions. But this limited perspective leaves so much on the table. Why settle for just avoiding harm when we can aim for so much more?

True recovery is about rediscovery—reclaiming the parts of yourself that have been lost along the way. It's about building a life so rich, meaningful, and fulfilling that the pull of addictive behaviors naturally weakens. When we take the science of flourishing and apply it to recovery, we unlock tools to:

- **Rewire the brain** with healthier habits and thought patterns (neuroscience, CBT, ACT).

- **Replace avoidance** with purpose and engagement (positive psychology, logotherapy).

- **Reconnect** to what truly matters: relationships, health, joy, and meaning.

- **Reshape resilience** so that setbacks become stepping stones, not barriers.

A Science-Backed Approach to Thriving

Imagine recovery not as the end of a struggle, but as the beginning of something extraordinary—a chance to build a life that feels whole, aligned, and worth living. That's the promise of this new vision for recovery:

- From neuroscience, we learn how the brain's reward system can be rewired for lasting habits and joy.

- From CBT and ACT, we gain tools to challenge unhelpful thoughts, regulate emotions, and take action in ways that serve us.

- From positive psychology, we discover the keys to human flourishing—resilience, gratitude, purpose, and connection.

- From happiness studies, we learn how to create sustainable well-being, moving beyond avoidance toward a life of thriving.

CHAPTER 2: REDEFINING RECOVERY

This is the foundation for **redefining recovery**—not as a reaction to crisis, but as a proactive journey toward reclaiming the best version of yourself. It's about taking the science of human flourishing and applying it to rebuild your life in ways that feel powerful, hopeful, and lasting.

Why wait until rock bottom to embrace this process? Why not start now, wherever you are, and use the tools that science and research have proven to help us thrive?

Let this chapter be your guide into a new way of seeing recovery. You're not just breaking free from something—you're moving *toward* something better: a life of well-being, balance, and fulfillment.

Let's explore what's possible when you embrace the science of flourishing and rediscover your capacity to live a life that feels deeply, richly, and truly yours.

With this vision in mind, the RECOVERY principles offer a roadmap—grounded in science, resilience, and hope—to help you create a life where addictive behaviors no longer have a hold. Each principle is a building block for thriving, showing you how to move from surviving to flourishing.

Introducing the RECOVERY Principles: Your Roadmap to Flourishing

Recovery is not just about stopping destructive patterns; it's about building a life so rich in joy, purpose, and connection that those patterns lose their hold. This is where the **RECOVERY principles** come in—a set of guiding pillars rooted in science, positive psychology, and behavioral change that help you move from surviving to thriving.

Each principle acts as a building block for lasting well-being, providing you with tools to:

- Rebuild your resilience and emotional strength.
- Replace harmful habits with healthier, life-affirming choices.
- Reconnect with your values, relationships, and purpose.

Think of the RECOVERY principles as both a foundation and a bridge—offering you steady support as you move away from addictive behaviors and toward a life of flourishing. Each principle is designed to address different areas of well-being, helping you recalibrate and realign your life in manageable, actionable ways.

Why These Principles Work

The RECOVERY principles aren't just ideas; they're backed by research and practical application. From neuroscience to positive psychology, from behavioral science to mindfulness practices, these principles draw on what truly works to help people heal, grow, and thrive.

Recovery isn't a one-size-fits-all process, and it doesn't happen overnight. But by incorporating these principles into your daily life—one step at a time—you'll create momentum toward meaningful, lasting change. Whether you're looking to break free from harmful patterns, recalibrate areas of your life, or simply rediscover what brings you joy and purpose, the RECOVERY principles will guide you.

What the Principles Offer

1. **A Clear Path Forward**: Each principle gives you practical tools to help you replace destructive behaviors with habits that align with your goals.

2. **Wholistic Growth**: These principles address your whole well-being- mind, body, and spirit,- helping you build a life that feels whole and balanced.

3. **Sustainable Change**: By focusing on small, meaningful steps, you'll lay the groundwork for habits and mindsets that support long-term recovery and well-being.

What Does RECOVERY Stand For?

Each letter in the word **RECOVERY** represents a principle that will help you break free from addictive behaviors and move toward a life of flourishing:

R **Resilience and Growth**: Strengthening your ability to bounce back from setbacks and using challenges as opportunities to grow.

E **Empathy and Self-Compassion**: Learning to treat yourself with kindness instead of shame, making change more sustainable and meaningful.

C **Connection and Positive Relationships**: Building supportive bonds that provide emotional grounding and reduce isolation.

O **Optimism and Gratitude**: Cultivating a mindset that focuses on the good, helping you find hope and motivation even in difficult moments.

V **Vitality and Health**: Prioritizing your physical and emotional well-being through movement, nutrition, and self-care.

E **Engagement and Purpose**: Immersing yourself in meaningful activities that bring joy and fulfillment, giving you a sense of direction.

R **Reflection and Mindfulness**: Staying present, observing triggers, and responding intentionally instead of reacting impulsively.

Y **You-Focused Empowerment**: Reclaiming your personal power, aligning your actions with your values, and creating a life that feels authentically yours.

CHAPTER 2: REDEFINING RECOVERY

How to Approach These Principles

Think of these principles as tools in your recovery toolbox. You don't need to master them all at once. Start with one principle that resonates most with you right now—maybe it's building resilience, fostering connection, or practicing mindfulness. Small steps add up, and each principle reinforces the others.

For example:
- Struggling with stress? Start with **Resilience and Growth**, learning how to face challenges without falling back on harmful habits.
- Feeling isolated? Lean into **Connection and Positive Relationships** to build a support network that encourages and uplifts you.
- Feeling stuck or uninspired? Explore **Engagement and Purpose** to reignite activities that bring meaning and joy to your life.

The beauty of the RECOVERY principles lies in their flexibility—they meet you where you are and help you take small, manageable steps forward.

A Promise of Hope

These principles are not just about avoiding pain; they're about creating a life worth living. A life that feels aligned with your values. A life where joy, connection, and purpose replace struggle and isolation.

You don't need to wait for rock bottom to start this journey. You don't need to have all the answers today. What matters is taking the first step—toward healing, growth, and rediscovery. The RECOVERY principles are here to guide you every step of the way.

Final Summary

Recovery is not just about breaking free from addictive patterns—it's about creating a life worth living. By shifting the focus from avoidance to thriving, this chapter explored how well-being can become the foundation for lasting change. Grounded in the science of human flourishing, positive psychology, and neuroscience, recovery becomes a process of rediscovery, growth, and empowerment. It's not about fixing what's broken, but about building what's possible: a life rich in joy, connection, and purpose. The RECOVERY principles are your guide to move beyond survival and into a thriving life where addictive behaviors no longer have a hold.

Key Takeaways

Recovery Is About Moving Toward, Not Just Away
Recovery is not just avoiding harmful habits but actively creating a life so fulfilling that addictive behaviors lose their pull. By building resilience, nurturing positive relationships, and rediscovering purpose, you focus on what you gain, not what you give up.

The Brain Is Wired for Growth
Thanks to neuroplasticity, your brain can unlearn harmful patterns and replace them with healthier, more intentional choices. Recovery is about rewiring these pathways—building new habits that align with your values and well-being.

Well-Being Is the Foundation for Lasting Change
The principles of human flourishing—resilience, connection, gratitude, mindfulness, and purpose—are not just ideas; they're practical tools. They give you the strength, clarity, and motivation to thrive, turning recovery into a journey of possibility.

A SPARK of HOPE

This journey is not about perfection—it's about progress, one small step at a time. Recovery isn't just the absence of struggle; it's the creation of something better. You are not defined by your past patterns or habits. You are capable of growth, of change, and of building a life that feels meaningful, joyful, and whole.

Every choice you make—no matter how small—is a step toward the person you want to be and the life you want to live. Trust the process. Trust yourself. Recovery isn't the end of the story—it's the beginning of a new chapter where you thrive. You are stronger than you think, and you are never alone on this path.

What sparked your curiosity or caught your attention?
(Reflect on what you found interesting or intriguing.)

_____
_____
_____
_____
_____

What insights or ideas feel actionable or relevant to your life?
(Identify what you can apply or implement.)

_____
_____
_____
_____
_____

What resonated deeply or felt personally meaningful to you?
(Consider what moved or inspired you emotionally or intellectually.)

_____
_____
_____
_____
_____

The RECOVERY Sunshine Assessment: Illuminate Your Path to Well-Being

Welcome to the RECOVERY Sunshine Assessment, a reflective tool designed to offer you a snapshot of how brightly your life is shining. Imagine your life as a radiant sun, with each principle of RECOVERY forming a ray of light. This exercise helps you visualize your strengths and identify areas for growth, empowering you to take intentional steps to enhance your well-being and recovery.

This isn't about judgment or perfection—it's about cultivating awareness, creating a snapshot and celebrating progress. By regularly using the RECOVERY Sunshine Assessment, you can track your journey and nurture a brighter, more balanced life.

How to Use the RECOVERY Sunshine Assessment

1. Draw Your Sunshine

On a piece of paper, draw a circle in the center to represent your core self. Alternatively, you can download the official Sunshine Assessment tool directly from our website at: www.readyforrecovery.life.

Around the circle, draw eight rays extending outward, labeling each with one of the RECOVERY principles:

2. Reflect and Rate (Ascribe) Each Ray

Consider the following questions for each principle to guide your reflection. Rate each area on a scale of 1 to 10:

1 = This area feels dim, neglected, or needs attention.
10 = This area feels vibrant, flourishing, and aligned.

Questions for Each Principle:

Resilience and Growth
- How well do I bounce back from challenges?
- Do I see setbacks as opportunities to grow?

Empathy and Self-Compassion
- Am I kind to myself during difficult times?
- Do I treat myself with the same understanding I would offer a friend?

Connection and Positive Relationships
- Do I feel supported by and connected to the people around me?
- Am I nurturing relationships that matter most?

Optimism and Gratitude
- Do I focus on what's good in my life, even during tough times?

- How often do I practice gratitude and notice positive moments?

Vitality and Health
- Am I taking care of my physical health through proper sleep, nutrition, and movement?
- Do I feel energetic and balanced in my daily life?

Engagement and Purpose
- Am I immersed in activities that bring me joy and fulfillment?
- Do I feel connected to a sense of purpose or meaning?

Reflection and Mindfulness
- How often do I pause to reflect on my thoughts, feelings, and actions?
- Am I present in the moment, or do I feel distracted or reactive?

You-Focused Empowerment
- Do I feel in control of my choices and direction?
- Am I living in alignment with my values and goals?

3. Connect the Rays

- Mark your rating along each ray, with **1** closest to the center and **10** at the tip.

- Connect the points to form a shape within your sunshine, representing the current brightness and balance of your well-being.

4. Reflect on (Describe) Your Sunshine

- **Bright Rays:** Which areas shine the brightest? Celebrate these strengths as pillars of your recovery journey.

- **Dim Rays:** Which areas feel dim or need nurturing? Describe why you gave yourself that ranking? These represent opportunities for growth.

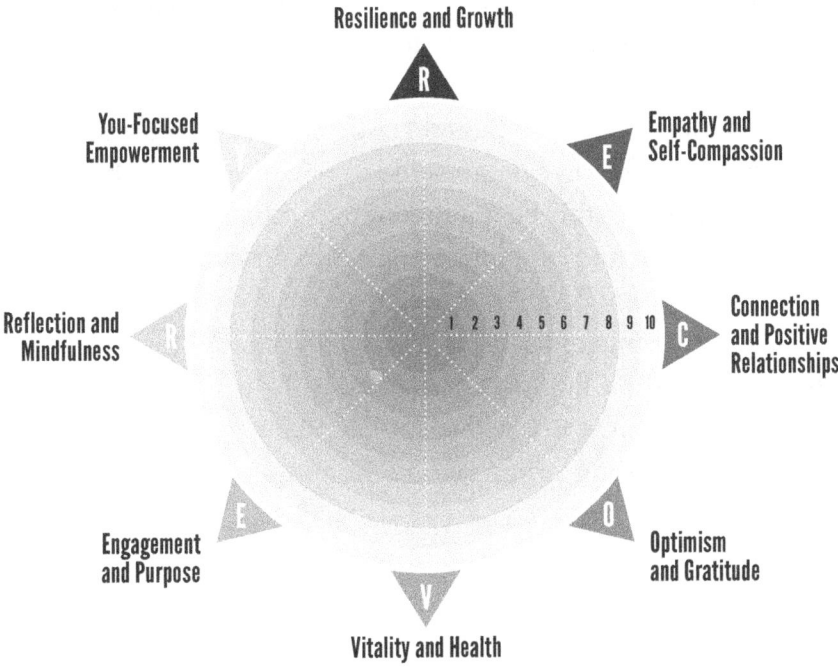

© Andrea Seydel 2025. www.readyforrecovery.life

Moving Toward Balance and Brilliance (Prescribe)

Ask yourself:
- What small steps can I take to brighten the dim rays and create a more balanced sunshine?

- How can I continue building on my brightest rays to strengthen my overall well-being?

- Using the insights and information you've gained from this assessment, take some time to reflect on the areas where balance could bring more harmony into your life. Feel free to jot down your thoughts, ideas, or actionable steps to brighten the rays of sunshine in one or more of these principles. Let this be a moment to nurture growth, restore equilibrium, and illuminate your path forward.

By regularly engaging with the RECOVERY Sunshine Assessment, you'll illuminate a clearer path to a vibrant, fulfilling recovery journey. Let this tool be your guide to nurturing balance, celebrating progress, and shining brighter with every step forward.

RECOVERY SUNSHINE ASSESSMENT

Resilience and Growth
_____
_____

Empathy and Self-Compassion
_____
_____

Connection and Positive Relationships
_____
_____

Optimism and Gratitude
_____
_____

Vitality and Health
_____
_____

Engagement and Purpose
_____
_____

Reflection and Mindfulness
_____
_____

You-Focused Empowerment
_____
_____

"What lies behind us and what lies before us are tiny matters compared to what lies within us."

– Ralph Waldo Emerson

PART 2

THE RECOVERY PRINCIPLES

CHAPTER 3

Resilience and Growth

Every challenge you face carries the seeds of growth within it. Resilience isn't about avoiding hardship—it's about meeting it with courage and intention. It's the quiet strength that allows you to adapt, recover, and choose well-being over temporary relief. Growth happens not in perfect moments but in imperfect ones—when you decide, again and again, to move forward. This chapter invites you to see your resilience as a foundation for transformation and your growth mindset as a gateway to lasting change. Together, they empower you to rise from every setback and move closer to the life you truly want.

RESILIENCE AND GROWTH

***"You are always one decision away
from a totally different life."*** *– Unknown*

Recovery is not a straight path, nor is it a one-time event. It is a journey of resilience and growth, a process of learning to rise stronger each time life challenges you. This chapter invites you to explore the immense power of your mind—your greatest tool for transformation. Through intentional decisions, psychological flexibility, and the nurturing voice of your Inner Encourager, you have the capacity to overcome addictive behaviors and build the life you envision. Let this be the chapter where you pivot, shifting from the patterns of the past to the possibilities of the future, and choose to empower your journey toward change.

Every moment holds a choice—a chance to align your actions with the life you want to create. Recovery begins with that choice. Resilience and growth are not about avoiding setbacks but about using them as stepping stones to rise stronger. This chapter explores how the **power of your mind** can help you overcome addictive behaviors by strengthening your resilience, shifting your mindset, and empowering your decisions.

Addictive behaviors often stem from a desire to cope with challenges, discomfort, or unmet needs. They might have served a purpose in the past, but they no longer align with the future you want. By harnessing your mind's ability to adapt, grow, and decide, you can replace these behaviors with healthier ways of navigating life's difficulties.

Resilience: The Power to Choose Well-Being

Resilience is your inner strength—the kind that allows you to make choices that prioritize your well-being, even when life gets tough. Think of it as your personal guide, helping you step away from addictive behaviors that no longer serve you and toward the life you want. Resilience doesn't erase the struggles of recovery, but it equips you with what you need to navigate them and bounce back stronger.

At its heart, resilience is about recognizing your capacity for growth and transformation. It's what helps you break free from the cycle of impulsive habits by offering clarity, courage, and the determination to stick to your goals. For example, research by Angela Duckworth on grit reminds us that perseverance through challenges is often what creates lasting change. Each time you choose your long-term well-being over the fleeting relief of an old habit, you're strengthening this muscle and reinforcing your commitment to a better path.

This journey begins with a single decision—choosing to lean into your resilience and the power of your mind. With every choice you make to step away from what holds you back, you're building the strength to face life's challenges and create a future rooted in freedom and well-being. As Carol Dweck's work on the growth mindset suggests, resilience isn't just about enduring; it's about believing in your ability to adapt and thrive.

Your Psychological Immune System: A Foundation for Resilience

Your mind has a remarkable capacity to protect and heal itself, often described as your psychological immune system. Just as your physical immune system fights off illness, this internal mechanism helps you adapt to stress, recover from setbacks, and thrive in the face of adversity. Renowned psychologist Dan Gilbert highlights this concept, explaining how our minds are wired to help us rebound from life's challenges, even when they feel overwhelming.

This system allows you to bounce back from difficulties, giving you the resilience to face them head-on. Every time you make a choice that aligns with your values—rather than giving in to impulsive or harmful behaviors—you reinforce this system. Growth and healing don't happen in giant leaps; they come from these small, meaningful decisions that add up over time.

The Role of Addictive Behaviors
In the past, you may have relied on addictive behaviors to shield yourself from discomfort, stress, or emotional pain. Or maybe these habits started out of curiosity or as a way to fit in socially. For instance, you might have picked up vaping to manage anxiety or turned to endless scrolling through social media as a way to escape feelings of boredom or overwhelm.

While these behaviors may have provided temporary relief or pleasure, they often carry hidden costs that add up over time—impacting your mental, physical, and emotional well-being. If you've made it this far into this book, it's because you're ready to confront those costs and take your life back from the grip of these habits.

Addictive behaviors can feel like a buffer, offering temporary stability during turbulent times. But true resilience comes from recognizing that you have the strength to face life's challenges without leaning on these crutches. Every time you choose well-being over an impulse, you strengthen your psychological immune system and take one step closer to the life you truly want.

Even when it feels like addictive behaviors have the upper hand, remember this: you already have the mental toughness and resilience within you to regain control. The power is yours to harness, one intentional choice at a time.

Psychological Flexibility: A Key to Resilience and Recovery
Psychological flexibility is the ability to stay present, open to experiences, and committed to actions that align with your values—even when faced with discomfort. This skill, a cornerstone of Acceptance and Commitment Therapy (ACT), plays a vital role in overcoming addictive behaviors. Research by Hayes, Strosahl, and Wilson (2011) highlights how enhancing psychological flexibility improves recovery outcomes, helping individuals handle temptations, stress, and challenging emotions without falling back into destructive habits.

Instead of avoiding discomfort, psychological flexibility empowers you to embrace challenges as opportunities for growth. It allows you to step back from immediate reactions, fostering resilience and keeping you grounded in your goals.

The Role of Psychological Flexibility in Building Resilience
Psychological flexibility and resilience are like two sides of the same coin, working together to form a protective buffer against adversity. Resilience helps you bounce back from setbacks, while psychological flexibility ensures you stay open to growth and learning, even in the face of difficulty.

When temptations or emotional triggers arise, psychological flexibility offers a three-step framework:

1. Observe: Notice the discomfort without judgment.
2. Accept: Recognize it as a normal part of the human experience.
3. Act: Choose a response that aligns with your recovery goals.

By practicing these steps, you reduce impulsive reactions, gain clarity, and foster long-term well-being.

Cognitive Restructuring: Taming Negative Thoughts
Automatic Negative Thoughts (ANTs) can undermine your confidence and make challenges feel insurmountable. Cognitive restructuring is a practical tool that helps you identify, challenge, and reframe these thoughts into empowering beliefs.

Steps to Restructure Thoughts:
1. Pause and Notice: Write down the negative thought (e.g., "I can't handle this").
2. Question the Thought: Examine its accuracy and challenge its validity.
3. Reframe It: Replace it with a constructive belief (e.g., "I've faced tough situations before, and I can handle this too").

4. Reflect on the Impact: Notice how this shift creates space for healthier choices.

Why Psychological Flexibility Matters in Recovery
Psychological flexibility allows you to adapt to life's unpredictability without being derailed by discomfort. By choosing actions that align with your values and long-term goals, you reduce the likelihood of relapse and enhance your overall well-being.

Integrating tools like cognitive restructuring and reframing setbacks strengthens your "psychological immune system," a concept introduced by Dan Gilbert (2006). This internal resilience helps you navigate emotional triggers and temptations with clarity and confidence.

Recovery isn't about avoiding discomfort; it's about learning to respond to it with intention. Each time you practice psychological flexibility, you strengthen your ability to move forward with purpose and resilience.

The Growth Mindset: A Catalyst for Change

A growth mindset is the empowering belief that you can learn, grow, and improve through effort and perseverance. When applied to overcoming addictive behaviors, it shifts your perspective from seeing these habits as insurmountable barriers to viewing them as opportunities to better understand yourself and build strength.

With a growth mindset, you can reframe your recovery journey. Instead of saying, "I can't change this habit," you can remind yourself, "I am learning how to make choices that serve me better." This subtle yet powerful shift contributes to resilience, allowing you to see setbacks not as failures but as stepping stones to progress. It's a reminder that the power to change lies in your perspective and your willingness to keep trying.

How a Growth Mindset Helps Overcome Addictive Behaviors
- **Reframes Challenges:** Addictive behaviors become opportunities for growth and self-discovery.
- **Fosters Belief in Change:** You recognize that improvement is possible, even if it takes time.
- **Builds Resilience:** A growth mindset helps you bounce back from slip-ups with determination, recalibration, and recommitment to your goals.

Your growth mindset works in tandem with your psychological immune system, equipping you with the tools to adapt, recover, and make intentional choices that align with your values and long-term goals.

Reframing Setbacks as Growth Opportunities

Setbacks are not failures—they are moments of learning.

- **Recognize Setbacks as Part of the Process:** Challenges are an inevitable part of life and recovery.

- **Identify Lessons:** What triggered the setback? How did you respond? What could you do differently next time?

- **Focus on Growth:** Use each challenge to gain insight and strengthen your resilience.

As Kristin Neff (2003) emphasizes, self-compassion plays a key role in growth. Treat yourself with kindness during these moments, understanding that missteps are natural and valuable parts of the journey.

Resilience, Growth, and Reclaiming Your Life

Every time you choose to reframe a setback as a growth opportunity, you reinforce your psychological immune system. With each positive decision, you strengthen your ability to adapt, recover, and thrive. Paired with a growth mindset, this resilience becomes an invaluable ally, helping you reclaim your life from addictive behaviors.

Each small step forward builds the foundation for a life that aligns with your values, free from habits that no longer serve you. Growth is not about perfection—it's about progress, and every effort you make brings you closer to the person you aspire to be.

Addictive Behaviors: Unmasking the Deeper Needs

Addictive behaviors often mask deeper emotions or unmet needs. It's not always easy to pinpoint why we turn to these behaviors, but they often provide temporary relief from stress, boredom, anxiety, loneliness, or even feelings of inadequacy.

For a brief moment, they can create a sense of control, distract us from pain, or fill an emotional void. For example, scrolling endlessly through social media or binge-watching Netflix might help avoid feelings of loneliness, while vaping might offer a fleeting sense of calm during overwhelming moments.

However, these behaviors ultimately keep us stuck in patterns that prevent growth and well-being. Instead of addressing the root causes of discomfort, addictive behaviors perpetuate cycles of dependency and self-sabotage, leaving underlying issues unresolved. They may feel helpful in the short term, but their long-term impact often includes physical, emotional, and relational harm. Recognizing this dynamic is a critical step in recalibrating away from these habits.

The Role of Mental Toughness

Mental toughness is the ability to stay focused, disciplined, and resilient when faced with challenges. It's about recognizing discomfort not as a barrier but as part of the process of change. When applied to addictive behaviors, mental toughness empowers us to acknowledge the temptation, pause to reflect, and make choices that align with our long-term goals instead of succumbing to immediate gratification.

One powerful strategy for building mental toughness is to first identify why we engage in addictive behaviors. By uncovering the emotions, unmet needs, or triggers that drive these habits, we can better understand their role in our lives and explore alternative ways to meet those needs.

The second step is to examine the costs of these behaviors—the negative impacts they have on our health, relationships, finances, and self-esteem. This awareness not only provides clarity but also fuels our determination to change. When we vividly connect with the downsides of these behaviors, it strengthens our resolve to take action—whether that means cutting back, quitting, or replacing the behavior entirely.

Awareness as the Foundation for Change

Awareness is the first step toward transformation. When we understand why we engage in addictive behaviors and the toll they take, we're better equipped to recalibrate and make intentional decisions. Mental toughness comes from this awareness, enabling us to confront discomfort, commit to change, and build a life aligned with our values and goals.

By exploring the reasons behind our behaviors and weighing their costs, we empower ourselves to take ownership of our actions. This process helps us break free from cycles of dependency and move toward healthier, more fulfilling alternatives. In the following section, we'll delve deeper into these dynamics and the role resilience plays in creating lasting change.

Understanding Your Why: Building Awareness of Addictive Behaviors

Resilience begins with self-awareness. To create lasting change, it's crucial to understand why you turn to addictive behaviors.

These habits don't happen in a vacuum—they often serve a purpose, whether it's to temporarily manage stress, escape discomfort, or fill an emotional void.

Psychologist Johann Hari famously said, "The opposite of addiction is not sobriety; it is connection." While this points to the importance of relationships, it also highlights the deeper needs—like belonging, purpose, or relief—that addictive behaviors may temporarily meet. By identifying these needs, you can begin to address them in healthier, more supportive ways.

Recognizing the "why" behind your habits is a transformative step. It shifts your focus from blaming yourself to understanding yourself, laying the foundation for resilience and intentional change.

Common Reasons for Addictive Behaviors

Addictive behaviors often stem from underlying emotional, psychological, or social needs. Here are some common reasons why people turn to these habits:

Emotional Coping
- **Stress Relief:** To manage overwhelming stress from work, relationships, or life challenges.
- **Anxiety Reduction:** To temporarily calm anxious thoughts or feelings.
- **Avoiding Sadness:** To numb feelings of sadness, loneliness, or depression.

- **Escaping Trauma:** To avoid reliving painful memories or experiences.

Avoidance of Discomfort
- **Avoiding Difficult Emotions:** To escape feelings like guilt, shame, or anger.
- **Escaping Reality:** To disconnect from problems, responsibilities, or overwhelming situations.
- **Boredom:** To fill a void or pass time without deeper engagement.

Seeking Pleasure or Reward
- **Instant Gratification:** To experience a quick boost of pleasure or a "high."
- **Routine Enjoyment:** To maintain a sense of comfort or familiarity tied to the behavior.
- **Dopamine Release:** To stimulate the brain's reward system and feel temporarily happier.

Sense of Control
- **Regaining Control:** To feel in charge of something when other areas of life feel chaotic.
- **Managing Uncertainty:** To create predictability or structure in unpredictable situations.

Social Factors
- **Peer Pressure:** To fit in or feel accepted by a group.
- **Cultural Norms:** Behaviors like drinking or smoking may be normalized in certain social or cultural contexts.

- **Loneliness:** To create a sense of connection or to fill the void of isolation.

Learned Behavior
- **Habitual Coping Mechanism:** Learned over time as a way to deal with life's challenges.
- **Modeling:** Witnessing family or friends use similar behaviors as coping strategies.

Physical Factors
- **Dependence:** To avoid withdrawal symptoms after physical dependency develops.
- **Fatigue Relief:** To increase energy or avoid feelings of exhaustion.

Self-Esteem or Identity
- **Boosting Confidence:** To feel more confident in social or personal settings.

- **Avoiding Self-Criticism:** To temporarily quiet negative self-talk or judgment.

Other Reasons
- **Trauma Response:** As a way to cope with unprocessed trauma or PTSD.
- **Curiosity:** Initially exploring out of curiosity, leading to habitual use.
- **Unmet Needs:** To compensate for unmet emotional or physical needs, such as feeling valued or loved.

How This Awareness Builds Resilience

Understanding why you engage in addictive behaviors gives you the tools to strengthen your resilience. By identifying the emotional, physical, or social needs these habits fulfill, you can begin to address those needs in healthier, more sustainable ways.

Resilience is about adapting, growing, and making intentional choices, even in the face of discomfort. Psychologist Carol Dweck, known for her work on the *growth mindset*, reminds us that challenges are not roadblocks—they're stepping stones for growth. When you uncover the deeper reasons for your behaviors, you're better equipped to reframe them as opportunities rather than obstacles. This awareness also empowers you to align your actions with your values and long-term goals, fostering meaningful progress.

Reflection Exercise: Exploring Your Why

Take a moment to reflect deeply on your own experiences with addictive behaviors. This exercise is about uncovering the underlying reasons behind your actions, helping you build awareness and create a foundation for meaningful change.

Questions to Reflect On:

Why do I engage in this behavior?
- What emotions, situations, or triggers lead me to this habit?

What needs am I trying to meet?
- Am I seeking comfort, distraction, or a sense of relief?

Am I avoiding discomfort or difficult emotions?
- What feelings or situations am I trying to escape from?

Am I searching for control, connection, or a way to cope?
- Does this behavior make me feel temporarily in control, less lonely, or more capable of handling stress?

Write your responses in a journal or on paper, being as honest and detailed as possible. This process will help you uncover the deeper needs behind your behaviors and set the stage for discovering healthier, more sustainable ways to meet them.

Uncovering the Hidden Costs of Addictive Behaviours

Every behavior comes with a cost, but addictive behaviors often carry hidden burdens that weigh on every aspect of life—physical, emotional, financial, and relational. Psychologist Daniel Kahneman's work on *loss aversion* highlights how we're often more motivated to avoid losses or negative costs than to seek gains. This exercise invites you to harness that insight by shining a light on the true impact of your addictive behaviors. By clearly seeing these consequences, you gain clarity about why these habits no longer serve you. This isn't about judgment—it's about awareness.

When you see the full picture, you empower yourself to make choices that align with your values, strengthen your resilience, and move closer to the person you want to become. Recognizing these costs is a courageous step toward intentional change. With this insight, you build the mental toughness to face discomfort, adapt to challenges, and choose healthier, more fulfilling ways to meet your needs. Let's uncover what's holding you back, so you can take the next step toward freedom and growth.

What Are the Costs?

Take the time to dig deep into the consequences of your addictive behaviors. This step is about uncovering all the ways these habits negatively impact your life. The more detail you can uncover, the more clarity you'll gain about why this behavior no longer serves you. This understanding can become a powerful motivator for change.

Ask Yourself:
How does this affect my health?
- Does it drain your energy or leave you feeling physically unwell?

- Are you experiencing chronic issues, such as poor sleep, weight changes, or a weakened immune system?

- Is it causing long-term damage, like respiratory problems, heart issues, or other conditions?

- Does it leave you feeling sluggish or unable to participate fully in life?

What toll does it take on my relationships or social life?
- Does this behavior cause tension, misunderstandings, or conflict with loved ones?

- Are you isolating yourself to engage in the behavior, leading to feelings of loneliness?

- Has it caused you to lose trust or respect from family or friends?

- Are you prioritizing the behavior over meaningful connections with others?

Does it hurt my finances or productivity?
- Are you spending more money than you can afford to sustain this habit?

- Has it created financial stress, such as debt or an inability to save for the future?

- Does it take time away from work or responsibilities, leading to missed opportunities or underperformance?

- Are you procrastinating or neglecting important tasks because of this behavior?

How does it affect my self-esteem or confidence?
- Do you feel ashamed or embarrassed about engaging in this behavior?

- Does it make you feel like you're not in control of your life or decisions?

- Have you lost confidence in your ability to change or accomplish goals?

- Do you feel like this behavior is holding you back from being the person you want to be?

Additional Questions to Consider:

How does this behavior impact my mental health?
- Does it contribute to feelings of anxiety, depression, or overwhelm?

- Are you using it to avoid or numb emotions instead of processing them?

Does it align with my values and goals?
- Does this behavior conflict with the person you want to be or the life you want to live?

- Is it keeping you from pursuing passions, hobbies, or meaningful activities?

How does it affect my future?
- Are there long-term consequences, such as health problems, strained relationships, or missed opportunities, that concern you?

- Is it holding you back from building the future you envision for yourself?

Why This Exercise Matters

These reflections are a powerful step toward understanding and transforming your behaviors. By uncovering the hidden dynamics behind your habits and the costs they carry, you set the stage for intentional change. Knowing this brings a resilience or mental toughness to your addictive behaviours. Recognizing these patterns builds your resilience—the ability to face discomfort, adapt, and grow stronger follow through on your determination to decrease or stop your additive behaviours. Each insight gained through this process enhances your capacity to make choices that align with your values, your goals for yourself and long-term well-being.

With clarity, you empower yourself to choose healthier ways to meet your needs and break free from patterns that no longer serve you. This exercise not only helps you identify what's holding you back but also nurtures your growth by showing you that change is not only possible, it's desirable.

The Power of Decision: Choosing Growth

At the heart of recovery lies the power of decision—the ability to choose a path that aligns with the person you want to become. Every moment presents an opportunity to take a step toward growth, well-being, and freedom from addictive behaviors. This journey begins with awareness and a commitment to change.

As Viktor Frankl, the renowned psychiatrist and Holocaust survivor, reminds us in *Man's Search for Meaning*, "Between stimulus and response there is a space. In that space is our power to choose our response. In our response lies our growth and our freedom." Recognizing that space is a cornerstone of recovery. It's where you reclaim your ability to choose intentionally, rather than react impulsively.

The first step on this resilient path is to recognize what your addictive behaviors have been providing for you. Perhaps they've offered temporary relief from pain, a sense of control, or a way to escape discomfort. Acknowledge these needs without judgment, as they help you understand the deeper reasons behind your habits. Once you identify these unmet needs, you can begin reframing your perspective and finding healthier, more sustainable ways to meet them.

The key to lasting change is making the costs of your addictive behaviors more tangible and emotionally impactful than the fleeting benefits they provide. This mental recalibration will guide your decisions and empower you to manage your behaviors effectively. By vividly connecting with the pain points—the damage to your health, relationships, or self-esteem—you create a powerful motivation to choose growth.

When your resilience is strengthened, and your mind is aligned with a growth mindset, change becomes the natural direction to move in. Remember, you have the power of your mind on your side. Through reflection, tapping into your resilience, and cultivating a growth mindset, you can make the decision to shift toward behaviors that support your well-being and the life you truly want.

In the previous exercise, you explored the ways your addictive behaviors might be supporting you and the costs they carry. Now, you'll take the next step—using this clarity to create a new calibration for your mind.

Reframing the Habit - *It's Not Worth It*

So far, you've explored the reasons why you might engage in addictive behaviors and identified the costs these habits have on your well-being. Now, it's time to revisit the balance between the benefits and costs of these behaviors to recalibrate your mindset.

For example:
- Benefit: "Smoking calms my anxiety in the moment."
- Cost: "It harms my lungs, drains my energy, and keeps me dependent on a substance for peace."

It's important to amplify the costs and fully connect with the pain points of your addictive behavior. Reflect deeply on how these habits affect your life, both now and in the future.

Ask yourself:
- How does this behavior hold me back from the life I want?
- What will happen if I continue this behavior for the next year? Five years? Ten years?
- What does it cost me emotionally, physically, and socially?

Take the time to write these thoughts down. The more vividly you can picture the consequences, the more powerfully they will motivate you to change.

The next step is to create a **reframing statement** to remind yourself that the costs of your addictive behavior outweigh the benefits. A well-crafted reframing statement acts as a powerful tool for lasting change, guiding you toward healthier choices and reinforcing your commitment to your goals.

When you feel tempted to engage in the behavior, use your reframing statement as an empowering reminder of the choice you're making to prioritize your well-being. This practice builds resilience and strengthens your ability to navigate urges with intention.

Here are some examples of reframing statements:
"This urge will pass, and I'll feel proud of myself for choosing something better."

"Engaging in this behavior takes me further away from my goals."

"I am stronger than this habit, and I deserve to feel free from it."

"I don't need this behavior to cope—I have healthier tools that truly support me."

"Each time I resist this urge, I build strength and resilience."

"This habit might provide temporary relief, but it's not worth the long-term cost to my health and happiness."

"Choosing growth over this behavior brings me closer to the person I want to be."

"This behavior no longer serves me; I choose actions that align with my values."

"I can handle this moment without turning to a habit that holds me back."

"True comfort comes from self-compassion, not from numbing myself with this habit."

Make Your Own Reframing Statement

Now it's your turn to craft a personalized reframing statement that resonates with your goals and values. Reflect on the costs you've identified and the life you envision for yourself. How can you remind yourself that the benefits of change far outweigh the temporary relief of old habits?

Take a moment to consider:
- What motivates you to move away from this behavior?

CHAPTER 3: RESILIENCE AND GROWTH

- What are the long-term benefits of choosing healthier actions?
- What empowering belief will help you navigate urges with intention?

Prompt:
Write your own reframing statement that you can turn to during moments of temptation. For example:

- "This behavior no longer serves me; I choose growth and freedom."

- "Every time I say no, I'm building the life I want."

Your Turn:

"My personalized reframing statement is:_____
_____
_____
_____."

Keep your statement simple, clear, and aligned with your goals. Write it down somewhere visible or save it on your phone as a reminder. Each time you use it, you're affirming your commitment to growth and reclaiming your power.

These reframing statements are powerful tools to help shift your mindset in the moment. They remind you of your strength, your values, and the intentional path you're walking toward a healthier and more fulfilling life. With every decision you make to resist an urge, you're reinforcing your resilience and empowering yourself to grow.

Creating a New Calibration: Reframing and Meeting Your Needs

Once you've identified the reasons behind your addictive behaviors and crafted a powerful reframing statement, it's time to take the next step. Look again at the needs these behaviors were fulfilling, but now from the perspective of finding alternative, healthier ways to meet those needs. This is where you reclaim your power by creating actionable strategies that align with your values and long-term goals.

Meeting your needs in healthier, alternative ways goes beyond simply avoiding addictive behaviors—it's about equipping yourself with the tools to face life's challenges with resilience and strength. Preparation is key, empowering you to adapt, grow, and navigate discomfort as it arises on your recovery journey. This process is deeply personal, as your choices should align with what genuinely supports your well-being and long-term goals. As you continue exploring the RECOVERY principles, you'll gain even more strategies and insights to strengthen your resilience and enhance your well-being. Here are some examples to inspire and guide you.

Examples of Alternative Actions to Meet Your Needs

If You Feel Stressed:
- Practice deep breathing exercises, like box breathing or 4-7-8 breathing.
- Do a quick meditation or mindfulness session using an app like Headspace or Calm.
- Engage in physical activity, like yoga, stretching, or a brisk walk.
- Write in a journal about what's causing your stress and brainstorm possible solutions.
- Create a calming ritual, such as lighting a candle or sipping herbal tea.
- Try progressive muscle relaxation to release tension in your body.

If You're Lonely:
- Call or video chat with a friend or family member.
- Join a social or hobby group, either in-person or online, to connect with others.
- Volunteer for a cause you care about to meet like-minded people.
- Start a creative project, like painting, knitting, or baking, and share it with someone.
- Take a pet for a walk or visit an animal shelter to spend time with animals.

If You're Bored:
- Explore a new area in your neighborhood or go for a scenic walk.

- Try a new recipe or experiment with cooking.
- Listen to a podcast or audiobook on a topic that sparks your curiosity.
- Learn a new skill, like drawing, coding, or playing a musical instrument.
- Organize or declutter a small space in your home to create a sense of accomplishment.

If You're Feeling Overwhelmed:
- Break tasks into smaller, manageable steps and tackle one at a time.
- Take a 10-minute "brain dump," writing down all your worries to clear your mind.
- Listen to calming music or nature sounds to create a soothing environment.
- Practice grounding exercises, such as focusing on your five senses.
- Step outside for fresh air and sunlight to reset your mood.

If You're Craving Comfort:
- Wrap yourself in a cozy blanket and watch a comforting movie or show.
- Take a warm shower or bath to relax your body and mind.
- Prepare a healthy, nourishing meal or snack and enjoy it mindfully.
- Practice self-compassion by writing affirmations or kind words to yourself.
- Do gentle yoga poses, like Child's Pose or Savasana, to ease tension.

If You're Feeling Anxious:
- Practice grounding techniques, like focusing on your breath or the present moment.
- Engage in a creative outlet such as drawing, coloring, or writing.
- Hold a stress ball, fidget toy, or another tactile object to channel nervous energy.
- Write down your worries and reframe them into constructive thoughts.
- Try aromatherapy with calming scents like lavender or chamomile.

If You're Feeling Disconnected or Numb:
- Take a nature walk and tune into the sights, sounds, and smells around you.
- Engage in an activity that stimulates your senses, like cooking, gardening, or playing music.
- Spend time connecting with others through shared activities or meaningful conversations.
- Journal about your feelings and explore ways to reconnect with yourself.
- Practice gratitude by listing three things you're thankful for in the moment.

If You're Seeking Validation or a Sense of Accomplishment:
- Set a small, achievable goal and complete it, like organizing a drawer or writing a to-do list.
- Acknowledge and celebrate progress in your recovery journey.
- Take on a new skill or challenge that builds confidence, like learning a recipe or trying a fitness goal.

- Help someone else by sharing your skills or supporting their needs.

If You're Feeling Triggered by a Relapse or Setback:
- Reach out to a support group, mentor, or trusted friend to talk about your feelings.
- Write down lessons learned from the experience and identify steps to move forward.
- Practice self-compassion and remind yourself that setbacks are a natural part of growth.
- Revisit your list of reasons for change and recommit to your goals.

By actively replacing your addictive behaviors with healthier alternatives, you're not only meeting your needs in a more sustainable way but also reinforcing your resilience. Each small action you take builds the mental strength needed to navigate challenges and strengthens your commitment to personal growth.

This process is a testament to your capacity to adapt and thrive. With each positive choice, you empower yourself to move closer to the life you want—one that aligns with your values and goals. Over time, these actions become habits, and these habits form the foundation of a resilient, growth-oriented mindset.

Your journey is unique, and the path forward is yours to create. By focusing on alternatives that support your well-being, you're transforming challenges into opportunities for growth and building a stronger, more fulfilling future.

Psychological Flexibility: Responding Instead of Reacting

Psychological flexibility is the ability to stay present, embrace discomfort, and make choices that align with your values. This flexibility allows you to be resilient and remain committed to the life you desire for yourself. It's about responding to challenges with intention rather than reacting impulsively.

Dr. Russ Harris, in *The Happiness Trap*, describes psychological flexibility as the cornerstone of well-being. He explains that learning to accept and engage with difficult emotions, rather than avoiding or fighting them, opens the door to making values-driven choices. This idea reinforces that discomfort doesn't need to derail you; it can be a signal to pause, reflect, and redirect.

Psychological flexibility encourages you to honor and accept emotions and challenges as they arise, embracing your humanness in the process. Accepting potential discomfort as part of the journey allows you to act in alignment with the decisions you've made for yourself. When the urge to engage in an addictive behavior arises—which it inevitably will—psychological flexibility helps you work with your thoughts and feelings. You can accept what's happening, adopt a growth mindset in the moment, and re-choose a better response for yourself.

Think of this practice like strengthening a muscle. Each time you choose to respond rather than react, you're building a habit of intentionality. The first few repetitions might feel awkward or even uncomfortable, but over time, the effort pays off in resilience and clarity.

This process takes repetition and practice. It's about consistently recommitting to your values and goals, even when it feels difficult. Revisit your list of the reasons and costs of your addictive behaviors and the alternatives you've identified to meet your needs. Create space for growth by practicing this cycle again and again.

How Psychological Flexibility Helps

When faced with a trigger or setback, psychological flexibility empowers you to:

Observe and Pause:
- Notice your thoughts and feelings without judgment.
- Take three deep breaths to ground yourself in the present moment.

Accept:
- Recognize that discomfort is temporary and part of the growth process.
- Practice self-acceptance by saying, *"This feeling will pass. I am stronger than this urge."*
- Use one of your powerful statements that you have created.

Choose:
- Respond in a way that supports your recovery and long-term goals.

- Take one small, intentional action, like journaling, calling a friend, or stepping outside for fresh air.

By practicing psychological flexibility, you strengthen your ability to navigate discomfort and stay aligned with your values. Over time, this practice helps you transform reactive patterns into intentional, value-driven choices.

Growth Mindset: Seeing Setbacks as Stepping Stones

A growth mindset empowers you to see challenges and setbacks not as failures, but as opportunities to learn, grow, and improve. It shifts your perspective from focusing on what went wrong to identifying what you can do better next time. Setbacks are a natural part of the journey—they don't define you; they refine you.

Think of setbacks as part of the learning curve rather than the finish line. With a growth mindset, each misstep becomes an opportunity to recalibrate and recommit to your goals. Remember, you're human, and slip-ups are part of the process. What matters most is how you choose to move forward.

Reframing Setbacks

The way you interpret a setback can make all the difference. Reframing allows you to shift from a fixed mindset, which sees mistakes as proof of failure, to a growth mindset, which views them as opportunities for development. Instead of thinking, "I slipped up, so I'll never succeed," you might tell yourself, "This setback is a chance to learn and strengthen my resilience."

 Try This: Learn and Grow Exercise

Reflect on a recent setback, using these prompts to guide your thoughts:

- What triggered the setback? Was it a stressful situation, an emotional state, or a specific environment?
- How did I respond, and what can I learn from this? Did the response align with my values?
- What might I do differently next time? Identify one actionable change you can make to handle similar situations in the future.

By reframing setbacks as stepping stones, you develop a mindset that embraces growth and resilience. Each slip-up becomes an opportunity to learn, adapt, and move closer to the life you want. Remember, progress is built one choice at a time.

Commit to Your New Path

Write a personal commitment statement that reflects your decision and choice to prioritize resilience, growth and well-being. Post it somewhere visible as a daily reminder.

Example Commitment Statements:

"I choose growth and well-being over temporary relief. Each decision I make brings me closer to the life I want."

"I am committed to prioritizing my well-being and making choices that align with the life I want to live."

"I choose to face challenges with courage and resilience, knowing that each step forward builds the future I deserve."

"I am stronger than my urges. My decisions today will create the freedom I seek tomorrow."

"I honor my growth by making choices that nurture my mind, body, and soul."

"Each time I choose resilience over impulse, I am reclaiming control of my life."

"I am capable of learning, growing, and overcoming. My choices today reflect the person I am becoming."

"I choose self-compassion and progress over perfection, knowing that small steps lead to big changes."

"I commit to embracing discomfort as part of my growth and turning it into strength."

"Every positive choice I make brings me closer to living authentically and free from behaviors that no longer serve me."

"I am in control of my choices. I am building a life aligned with my values and dreams."

This exercise helps you recalibrate your mindset by amplifying the costs of your behavior and shifting your focus toward healthier alternatives. With each choice, you strengthen your resilience, empower your mind, and align with the person you desire to be.

Chapter Summary

Resilience and growth are not about perfection but about progress. They are the foundations of transformation, empowering you to navigate life's challenges with strength, courage, and intention. Through cultivating resilience, embracing a growth mindset, and practicing psychological flexibility, you can reframe setbacks, meet your needs in healthier ways, and align your choices with the life you envision.

Your mind is your greatest ally in this journey. By understanding the costs of addictive behaviors, reframing your mindset, and nurturing your psychological immune system, you reclaim your power to adapt, recover, and thrive. Every step forward—no matter how small—is a testament to your resilience and a declaration of your commitment to growth. Trust in the process, knowing that each choice you make brings you closer to the person you are meant to be.

Key Takeaways

Resilience is a skill you can build: It acts as your psychological immune system, enabling you to rise after setbacks and face challenges with courage and intention. Every positive choice strengthens your ability to recover and adapt.

A growth mindset transforms setbacks into opportunities: By viewing challenges as stepping stones rather than roadblocks, you empower yourself to learn, grow, and build momentum toward lasting change.

Psychological flexibility supports lasting recovery: Staying present, accepting discomfort, and aligning your actions with your values allow you to navigate urges and triggers with clarity and resilience.

Understanding the costs of addictive behaviors amplifies motivation for change: Connecting deeply with the negative impact of these habits on your health, relationships, and future fuels your determination to choose healthier alternatives.

Reframing your mindset is a powerful tool for change: Personalized reframing statements help shift your focus from immediate urges to long-term goals, reinforcing your resilience and commitment to well-being.

Resilience and Growth Pulse Check

Reflecting on your progress with the **RECOVERY Sunshine Assessment**, take a moment to evaluate your current level of resilience and how it's influencing your recovery journey. Consider this a focused check-in on this particular ray of sunshine, offering insight into where you stand and where you can grow.

Ascribe

On a scale of 1–10, how resilient do you feel right now? Use these questions to guide your rating:

1. How do you usually respond to challenges or setbacks?
2. When faced with a recent difficult situation, how effectively did you bounce back?
3. Do you feel confident in your ability to handle discomfort or emotional triggers?
4. How often do you see setbacks as opportunities for growth?
5. To what extent do you rely on strategies like reframing or psychological flexibility to navigate tough moments?

Describe
- What recent challenges have tested your resilience?
- How did you respond to those challenges?
- What tools or strategies helped you bounce back?
- In what ways did you grow or learn from those experiences?

Prescribe

Identify one action you can take to strengthen your resilience:

- What's one small step you can take today to build your psychological flexibility or personal strength?
- How can you reframe a current challenge as an opportunity for growth?

Actionable Inspirations
Here are concrete ways to strengthen your resilience and reinforce the lessons from this chapter:

- Practice reframing a current setback as a stepping stone for personal growth. Ask, *What can I learn from this?*
- Set a small, achievable goal that aligns with your values and strengthens your sense of purpose.
- Write down three ways you've grown stronger after past challenges to remind yourself of your capacity to adapt.
- Use cognitive restructuring to challenge and reframe a negative thought into an empowering one. For example, change "I can't handle this" into "I've handled tough situations before, and I can do it again."
- Visualize your "resilient self" responding to challenges with strength and clarity. Use this image to guide your actions during moments of stress.

Sentence Completions
Deepen your self-awareness and strengthen your resilience with these prompts:

- *When I face challenges, I can rise stronger by…*
- *A time I bounced back from a setback was…*
- *I know I'm resilient because…*
- *To grow stronger, I will…*

Mantra for Resilience
"I rise after every fall, stronger and wiser than before."

Or create your own:
_____
_____
_____

A SPARK of HOPE

You have within you the strength to rise, even when it feels hard. Every choice you make to align with your values strengthens your resilience and brings you closer to the person you're becoming. Growth isn't about perfection—it's about progress, about taking one step at a time toward a brighter, freer future. Trust in your ability to adapt, learn, and rise stronger. You are capable, you are growing, and you are creating a life filled with strength and possibility. Keep going—you've got this.

What sparked your curiosity or caught your attention?
(Reflect on what you found interesting or intriguing.)

_____
_____
_____
_____
_____

What insights or ideas feel actionable or relevant to your life?
(Identify what you can apply or implement.)

_____
_____
_____
_____
_____

What resonated deeply or felt personally meaningful to you?
(Consider what moved or inspired you emotionally or intellectually.)

_____
_____
_____
_____
_____

CHAPTER 4

Empathy and Self-Compassion

When life feels heavy, and emotions seem overwhelming, it's tempting to push them aside or power through without stopping to listen. But what if the very emotions you avoid are the ones holding the keys to your resilience and growth? Empathy and self-compassion invite you to lean in, not turn away—to embrace your humanity and meet yourself with the same kindness you'd offer to a friend. This isn't about perfection or fixing everything at once; it's about creating space to understand, accept, and grow. As you go through this chapter, consider this an opportunity to strengthen the most important relationship in your life—the one with yourself.

EMPATHY AND SELF-COMPASSION

"With self-compassion, we give ourselves the same kindness and care we'd give to a good friend." – Kristin Neff

Imagine offering the same kindness and understanding to yourself that you readily give to others. Empathy and self-compassion are not just acts of self-care—they are profound tools for healing, growth, and resilience. By learning to meet your emotions with curiosity instead of judgment, you create space for self-awareness and transformation.

This chapter explores how empathy and self-compassion can deepen your connection to yourself, help you process emotions in a healthy way, and reduce the reliance on harmful coping mechanisms. You'll discover how these qualities not only nurture emotional balance but also build the foundation for a life aligned with your values and aspirations. Let this be an invitation to treat yourself with the same gentleness you would a dear friend, embracing your humanity while cultivating strength and growth.

Emotions: What They Are, Why They Matter, and the Consequences of Ignoring Them

Emotions shape every aspect of our lives, influencing decisions, relationships, and personal growth. While powerful and sometimes overwhelming, they are essential signals that guide us toward our needs, values, and well-being. However, in a world that often prioritizes logic over feelings, emotions are frequently misunderstood or ignored—a mistake that can fuel unhealthy coping mechanisms and stifle growth.

To thrive in recovery and beyond, we must understand what emotions are, why they matter, and the consequences of neglecting them.

What Are Emotions?

Emotions are like your body's personal messaging system, constantly delivering updates about what's happening both inside and around you. They're not just random reactions—they're purposeful signals designed to grab your attention and guide your actions. Each emotion has a specific job, offering valuable insights into your needs and experiences.

For example:
- **Fear:** This is your internal alarm, alerting you to potential danger and helping you prepare to respond.

- **Anger:** Think of it as your boundaries advocate, showing up when there's injustice or when your personal limits are being crossed.

- **Sadness:** This tender emotion highlights loss or unmet needs, inviting you to slow down and process what's important.

- **Joy:** Your body's way of throwing a little party, joy celebrates meaningful connections, achievements, or moments of fulfillment.

And that's just the beginning—your emotional spectrum is rich and nuanced, offering clues about your inner world. Emotions are like a navigation system, always working to steer you toward actions that protect, support, and enrich your life.

As Brené Brown beautifully puts it in her research on emotions, "We cannot selectively numb emotions; when we numb the painful emotions, we also numb the positive ones." Recognizing and understanding emotions is essential, not only for survival but also for cultivating connection, compassion, and growth.

Take a moment to consider how often your emotions are trying to communicate with you. By learning to listen and respond, you gain a deeper understanding of yourself and build the capacity to connect with others in meaningful ways. Emotions are not problems to be solved—they're messages to be received.

Why Emotions Matter

Emotions are not "good" or "bad"—they're simply part of being human, each carrying a valuable message. Instead of judging them, think of emotions as signposts, guiding you toward decisions and actions that align with your values and needs.

Here's how emotions play a crucial role in your life:

- **Decision-Making:** Emotions help you weigh risks, set priorities, and make choices that align with what truly matters. For example, excitement might signal a "yes," while hesitation could invite caution.

- **Connection:** They're the glue that fosters empathy, communication, and bonding with others. As Maya Angelou wisely noted, "People will forget what you said, people will forget what you did, but people will never forget how you made them feel."

- **Self-Understanding:** Reflecting on your emotions uncovers triggers, unmet needs, and values, deepening your self-awareness.

- **Resilience and Growth:** Even the hard-to-face emotions carry lessons, offering opportunities to learn, adapt, and grow.

When you acknowledge your emotions, you equip yourself with the tools to face life's challenges head-on. But when you suppress or ignore them, emotions often become the driving force behind destructive habits.

The Cost of Ignoring Emotions

Suppressing emotions doesn't make them disappear; it makes them louder, often in unhealthy ways:

- **Stress and Health Issues:** Bottled-up emotions can lead to chronic stress, anxiety, and even physical ailments like headaches or digestive problems.

- **Emotional Dysregulation:** Suppressed feelings have a sneaky way of resurfacing as outbursts, overwhelm, or unpredictable mood swings.

- **Addictive Behaviors:** When emotions like sadness, frustration, or boredom are ignored, addictive behaviors often step in as a way to numb or escape those feelings. Whether it's overeating, drinking, or compulsive scrolling, these habits become quick fixes for unprocessed emotions.

- **Relationship Strain:** Unaddressed emotions create barriers to connection, leading to misunderstandings and unresolved conflicts. This disconnection can further fuel the cycle of turning to addictive behaviors for comfort.

As Dr. Susan David, author of *Emotional Agility,* explains, "Discomfort is the price of admission to a meaningful life." Ignoring emotions might feel easier in the moment, but true resilience and connection come from acknowledging, understanding, and working with them.

By avoiding emotions, you risk staying stuck in a cycle where addictive behaviors become your go-to strategy for coping. Recognizing why emotions matter and the cost of ignoring them is a powerful step toward breaking that cycle. Honoring what you feel not only builds resilience but also reduces the pull of addictive behaviors, paving the way for healthier ways to navigate life's challenges.

Engaging with Emotions: A Practical Approach

Rather than avoiding emotions, treat them as valuable messengers guiding you toward greater self-awareness and growth. Engaging with emotions allows you to understand their messages and act intentionally. Here's how:

Pause and Notice
Take a moment to tune into your body. Pay attention to physical sensations tied to emotions—like tightness in your chest, warmth in your face, or butterflies in your stomach. Ask yourself, "What am I feeling right now?" Emotions often speak through your body before your mind catches up.

Name the Emotion
Naming your emotions helps diffuse their intensity and bring clarity. Neuroscientist Lisa Feldman Barrett explains that labeling emotions activates the brain's prefrontal cortex, giving you more control over your response. For example, you might realize sadness and anger are coexisting or that anxiety and excitement are intertwined.

Explore the Message
Emotions aren't random—they're signals prompting meaningful action. Consider these common emotions and their messages:

Anger: A boundary has been crossed. What action can you take to protect or restore your boundary?

Fear: There's uncertainty or danger. How can you prepare or seek safety?

Sadness: You've experienced a loss. What comfort or support would help you heal?

Joy: Something meaningful has happened. How can you savor and create more of this?

Guilt: Your actions may not align with your values. What can you do to make amends or realign?

Shame: You feel unworthy or inadequate. Are these feelings rooted in truth, or can you show yourself compassion and let go of unrealistic expectations?

Anxiety: You're facing uncertainty. What's within your control, and how can you calm yourself?

Gratitude: You're aware of life's positives. How can you express or expand this feeling?

Frustration: Obstacles are in your way. What adjustments can you make to move forward?

Loneliness: You need connection. Who can you reach out to for support?

Awe: You're inspired by something greater than yourself. How can you bring more wonder into your life?

Validate Your Feelings
Your emotions are valid, no matter what they are. Instead of thinking, "I shouldn't feel this way," remind yourself that emotions are

natural responses to your experiences. As Susan David, author of *Emotional Agility,* reminds us, "Emotions are data, not directives." They inform you, but they don't have to dictate your actions.

Respond Intentionally
Decide how to act in alignment with your values. For example, if anger signals a crossed boundary, you might choose to assertively communicate rather than lash out. Responding with intention fosters growth, while reacting impulsively often leads to regret.

Practice Regulation
If emotions feel overwhelming, grounding techniques can help create space for calm reflection:

- Take deep, measured breaths (like 4-7-8 breathing).
- Focus on your senses (e.g., "What do I see, hear, feel, taste, smell?").
- Practice mindfulness to anchor yourself in the present moment.

Reflect and Learn
Journaling can be a powerful tool to process emotions. Write about what you're feeling, the situation that triggered it, and what insights you can take away for the future. This practice deepens self-awareness and helps you recognize emotional patterns.

Emotions: Allies in Recovery

Emotions are not barriers—they're guides to healing and growth. Glennon Doyle beautifully states in *Untamed,* "Feelings are for feeling. All of them. Even the hard ones. The secret is that you're doing it right, and doing it right hurts sometimes." Listening to your emotions allows you to learn, adapt, and move closer to the life you want.

Engaging with emotions helps you:

- **Reduce Stress:** Address the root causes of stress rather than suppressing them.

- **Break Addictive Cycles:** Acknowledge and process emotions instead of numbing them.

- **Strengthen Relationships:** Share and communicate emotions to foster understanding and trust.

So, instead of asking, "How can I avoid this feeling?" try reframing the question: "What is this emotion teaching me?" Emotions are the bridge between where you are and the life you're striving to create.

Meeting Emotions with Self-Compassion and Empathy: Tools for Healing and Preventing Addictive Behaviors

Emotions shape every aspect of our lives—they guide decisions, deepen relationships, and influence how we view ourselves and the world. Yet, emotions often carry a stigma, leading us to suppress or judge them rather than embrace them as a natural part of being human. By meeting emotions with self-compassion and empathy, you can transform them into powerful tools for growth, resilience, and healing.

The Role of Compassion and Empathy in Emotional Wellness

Difficult emotions such as sadness, anger, and fear are often met with avoidance or criticism. However, psychologist Kristin Neff, a leading researcher on self-compassion, explains that avoiding or judging emotions only intensifies their grip, creating cycles of shame, disconnection, and unhealthy coping mechanisms. Instead, meeting emotions with compassion and empathy acknowledges their value and allows them to guide you toward healing.

Normalize the Human Experience: Emotions are not signs of weakness—they are universal and remind us of our shared humanity. As Brené Brown says, "We are hardwired for connection, and emotion is the language of connection."

Foster Healing: Self-compassion reduces anxiety, depression, and emotional distress by quieting the inner critic (Neff, 2003).

Enhance Emotional Regulation: Approaching emotions with empathy makes them easier to process, reducing impulsive reactions and fostering thoughtful responses.

The Costs of Suppressing or Judging Emotions

When emotions are ignored or judged, they don't disappear—they find other, often harmful, ways to surface. These consequences may include:

- **Shame and Isolation:** Harsh self-criticism amplifies feelings of inadequacy and disconnection.

- **Emotional Overflow:** Suppressed feelings often accumulate and erupt unexpectedly.

- **Unhealthy Coping Mechanisms:** Avoidance behaviors like overeating, overworking, or substance use frequently stem from unprocessed emotions (Kelly et al., 2018).

Cultivating Self-Empathy and Self-Compassion

What Are Self-Empathy and Self-Compassion?
Self-Empathy: The ability to tune into and validate your own emotions with curiosity and understanding.

Self-Compassion: Treating yourself with kindness, recognizing shared humanity, and observing your emotions without judgment (Neff, 2003).

Why They Matter
- **They Reduce Emotional Overload:** Self-compassion calms the inner critic and makes it easier to face challenges.

- **They Enhance Resilience:** Research shows self-compassion fosters adaptability and reduces emotional burnout (Germer & Neff, 2013).

- **They Break the Cycle of Avoidance:** Compassionately engaging with emotions reduces the need for harmful coping mechanisms (Kelly et al., 2018).

Practical Steps to Embrace Emotions with Compassion and Empathy

1. Acknowledge Your Emotions
Start by recognizing your feelings without judgment. Dr. Matthew Lieberman's research highlights that simply naming your emotions can reduce their intensity (Lieberman et al., 2007).

2. Practice Self-Kindness
Replace self-critical thoughts with compassionate ones. Instead of saying, "I shouldn't feel this way," try, "It's okay to feel this—it's part of being human."

3. Engage in Mindfulness
Stay present with your emotions using techniques like deep breathing or journaling. Mindfulness-based practices have been shown to improve emotional regulation and reduce distress (Hofmann et al., 2010).

4. Normalize Your Experience
Remind yourself that everyone experiences struggles. As Tara Brach notes in her book *Radical Acceptance,* "When we can touch our suffering with awareness and love, it transforms."

5. Reframe Setbacks
View challenges as opportunities for learning and growth rather than as failures.

How Compassion and Empathy Support Recovery

Addictive behaviors often stem from attempts to escape emotional discomfort. Embracing self-compassion allows you to engage with these emotions constructively:

Acknowledge Emotional Pain: Create space to process emotions instead of suppressing them.

Reduce Shame: Reframe guilt or self-criticism as opportunities for growth.

Build Resilience: Over time, meeting emotions with kindness strengthens your ability to navigate challenges.

For example, instead of reaching for a harmful coping mechanism, pause and ask yourself: *"What is this feeling trying to tell me, and how can I respond in a way that aligns with my values?"*

As Glennon Doyle reminds us in *Untamed*, "You can't keep choosing what doesn't change you." By meeting emotions with compassion and empathy, you allow them to become catalysts for healing and transformation, guiding you toward the life you truly want to live.

The Inner Encourager vs. the Inner Critic

The Inner Encourager vs. the Inner Critic
We all have inner voices that shape how we view ourselves and navigate challenges. Among these, two are especially impactful: the Inner Encourager, which fosters self-compassion and growth, and the Inner Critic, which amplifies self-doubt and judgment. Learning to amplify the voice of self-compassion through your Inner Encourager is key to transforming your relationship with emotions and fostering resilience in the face of addictive behaviors.

The Inner Encourager
Your Inner Encourager is the embodiment of self-compassion—a kind and understanding voice that supports you through life's ups and downs. It treats you as a close friend would, offering encouragement and reassurance when you need it most. This voice celebrates your progress, reminds you of your strengths, and motivates you to keep moving forward. It says things like:

"You're doing your best, and that's enough."
"This is hard, but you've faced challenges before and grown stronger each time."
"You can make choices that honor your well-being."

By practicing self-compassion, your Inner Encourager helps you approach challenges with kindness and understanding, reframing setbacks as learning opportunities rather than failures. This mindset not only strengthens your resilience but also aligns your actions with your values and long-term goals.

The Inner Critic
The Inner Critic, on the other hand, represents self-judgment and harshness. It often speaks from a place of fear or insecurity, discouraging you with messages like:

"You'll never get this right."
"You're not strong enough to resist."
"Why even try? You always fail."

The Inner Critic thrives on negativity, fueling cycles of shame and avoidance that make it harder to connect with your emotions and values. While this voice can feel overpowering, self-compassion allows you to quiet it by reminding yourself that mistakes are part of being human.

Connecting Self-Compassion to Your Inner Encourager
When you choose to listen to your Inner Encourager, you activate self-compassion by treating yourself with the same kindness and patience you'd offer a loved one. This voice reminds you to approach your emotions and challenges with curiosity, not criticism. It encourages you to validate your feelings and acknowledge your efforts without judgment.

Examples in Action
- **Inner Critic:** "You've failed so many times before; you'll never succeed."

- **Inner Encourager:** "Everyone stumbles—what matters is that you're learning and growing."

- **Inner Critic:** "You're too weak to resist this craving."
  Inner Encourager: "You've made strong choices before, and you can do it again. Each effort builds your resilience."

- **Inner Critic:** "Change is too hard—you'll never manage it."
  Inner Encourager: "Every small step matters. You're moving toward the life you deserve, and that's worth the effort."

Self-Compassion as a Path to Resilience
Tapping into your Inner Encourager is an act of self-compassion. It allows you to meet your struggles with empathy, understanding, and a focus on growth. By shifting your inner dialogue, you align with your values and build resilience in the face of challenges.

By meeting your Inner Critic with self-compassion, you quiet the judgment and foster a nurturing environment for growth. As Kristin Neff emphasizes, self-compassion isn't about avoiding challenges—it's about meeting them with the kindness and care you deserve. Let your Inner Encourager guide you toward resilience, recovery, and a life aligned with your values.

The Permission to Be Human: A Path to Emotional Healing and Growth

In a culture that often prioritizes perfection and control, giving yourself the "permission to be human" is an act of profound self-compassion and growth. This concept, coined by positive psychology pioneer Dr. Tal Ben-Shahar, invites you to embrace your humanity—your imperfections, emotions, and struggles—without judgment. It's not about excusing harmful behaviors but about meeting yourself with empathy and understanding as you navigate life's challenges.

What Does It Mean to Have Permission to Be Human?
The permission to be human recognizes that experiencing a full range of emotions is not a flaw but an essential part of living. Emotions—whether joy, sadness, anger, or fear—serve as signals, guiding you toward what matters in your life. Denying these emotions often leads to greater distress and reliance on unhealthy coping mechanisms (Gross, 2002).

Dr. Ben-Shahar reminds us that allowing yourself to feel—even the uncomfortable emotions—is key to building resilience and fostering growth. Embracing this concept means acknowledging imperfections while taking responsibility for your actions, creating a foundation for healing and self-awareness.

Why Permission to Be Human Matters
1. **It Reduces Emotional Suppression:**
   Research shows that suppressing emotions increases stress and mental health challenges (Gross, 2002). Acknowledging your feelings diminishes emotional pressure, reducing the need to numb or avoid them.

2. **It Supports Emotional Regulation:**
   Naming and understanding your emotions allows you to process them constructively, helping you respond thoughtfully instead of reacting impulsively (Neff, 2003).

3. **It Encourages Self-Compassion:**
   According to Dr. Kristin Neff, self-compassion nurtures resilience and reduces the harmful effects of self-criticism, creating space for healing and well-being.

4. **It Prevents Avoidance Behaviors:**
   Recognizing emotions eliminates the need for addictive behaviors by providing healthier ways to cope (Kelly et al., 2018).

Acceptance vs. Excusing Behavior

Granting yourself permission to be human doesn't mean justifying harmful actions—it's about understanding your emotions while taking responsibility for your choices.

- **Acceptance**: Recognizing emotions without judgment. Example: "I feel overwhelmed and want to escape. How can I address this constructively?"

- **Excusing Behavior**: Avoiding accountability. Example: "I was overwhelmed, so it's okay that I lashed out."

Acceptance leads to growth, while excusing behavior keeps you stuck in negative cycles.

How Permission to Be Human Helps With Addictive Behaviors

Addictive behaviors often emerge as an attempt to escape uncomfortable emotions. When you give yourself permission to feel, you open the door to healthier alternatives:

- **Allows Emotional Expression**: Recognizing your emotions prevents the emotional buildup that fuels harmful behaviors.

- **Creates Space for Reflection**: Naming emotions gives you a moment to pause, reflect, and choose actions aligned with your values.

- **Builds Resilience**: Over time, meeting your emotions with acceptance strengthens your ability to navigate them without resorting to unhealthy coping mechanisms.

Embrace Your Humanity
Giving yourself permission to be human is a transformative act of self-compassion. It allows you to accept your emotions, learn from your experiences, and grow through life's challenges. This simple yet profound shift creates a space for healing, resilience, and authentic living.

As Dr. Tal Ben-Shahar wisely said, *"Being human means being imperfect."* By embracing your imperfections and honoring your emotions, you take a step toward self-acceptance and open the door to meaningful change.

The Power of Acceptance and Commitment Therapy (ACT): A Path to Emotional Wellness

Acceptance and Commitment Therapy (ACT), developed by Dr. Steven C. Hayes, offers a transformative framework for embracing emotions, committing to values-driven actions, and building psychological flexibility. At its heart, ACT aligns beautifully with self-compassion, emphasizing the acceptance of emotions without judgment and guiding individuals toward a meaningful, value-centered life (Hayes et al., 2011).

What Is ACT?
ACT is grounded in six core processes that work together to cultivate psychological flexibility—the ability to adapt your behavior while staying true to your values:

Acceptance: Embrace emotions and thoughts instead of suppressing or avoiding them.

Cognitive Defusion: Observe your thoughts without being controlled by them.

Being Present: Stay mindful and engaged in the current moment.

Self-as-Context: Recognize that you are more than your emotions or thoughts.

Values: Identify what truly matters to you.

Committed Action: Take purposeful steps aligned with your values, even when it's uncomfortable (Hayes et al., 2011).

This approach shifts the focus from fighting negative emotions to learning from them, promoting resilience and personal growth.

How ACT Helps Prevent Addictive Behaviors
Addictive behaviors often arise as an escape from discomfort. ACT provides a roadmap to address this by combining acceptance and self-compassion. Through ACT principles, you can:

- **Acknowledge temptations without acting on them**: Recognize cravings as temporary experiences.

- **Accept discomfort as part of the process**: Normalize challenging emotions without judgment.

- **Align actions with values**: Choose responses that reflect your long-term goals rather than short-term relief.

For instance, when faced with stress, instead of turning to addictive behaviors, ACT encourages pausing, accepting the discomfort, and asking yourself, *"What action aligns with my values?"* This subtle yet powerful shift supports healthier responses and reinforces your commitment to recovery.

A Real-Life Example of ACT in Action
After a stressful day, ACT might guide you through the following process:

1. **Pause and Accept**: Acknowledge the stress without judgment. Example: *"This is hard, but it's okay to feel this way."*

2. **Defuse Negative Thoughts**: Reframe, *"I can't handle this,"* into, *"I'm having the thought that this is overwhelming, but I've handled tough situations before."*

3. **Act on Your Values**: If self-care is a core value, choose a constructive action like journaling, calling a friend, or going for a walk.

By responding this way, emotional challenges become opportunities for resilience and growth rather than triggers for harmful behaviors.

The Transformative Power of ACT
When combined with self-compassion and empathy, ACT fosters emotional balance and resilience. Together, these principles encourage you to:

- Accept emotions as natural parts of the human experience.
- Meet emotions with kindness and understanding.
- Commit to actions aligned with your values, even when it's difficult.

By integrating these practices, you can navigate life's challenges with greater ease, transforming them into pathways for personal growth and fulfillment. As Dr. Hayes reminds us, true emotional wellness doesn't come from avoiding discomfort but from living authentically, guided by your values and supported by acceptance (Hayes et al., 2011).

In embracing ACT, you're not just managing emotions—you're creating a life that aligns with who you truly are and who you aspire to be.

Chapter Summary

Empathy and self-compassion are cornerstones of emotional well-being and resilience. They empower you to embrace your humanity, including your imperfections and struggles, with kindness and understanding. By listening to your emotions, validating your experiences, and meeting challenges with curiosity rather than judgment, you lay the groundwork for healing and personal growth.

In this chapter, you've learned how to engage with emotions as messengers, offering valuable insights into your needs and values. You've explored practical tools to foster self-compassion, such as reframing setbacks, addressing your inner critic, and giving yourself the permission to be human. Acceptance and Commitment Therapy (ACT) complements this approach, providing a framework to embrace discomfort, commit to values-driven actions, and build psychological flexibility.

When you integrate empathy and self-compassion into your daily life, you reduce emotional suppression, strengthen resilience, and align your actions with the person you aspire to be. This journey is not about perfection but progress—each step, no matter how small, brings you closer to a life of authenticity, freedom, and fulfillment.

Key Takeaways

Emotions Are Messengers: Emotions, both positive and negative, are natural responses that guide you toward understanding your needs and values. By acknowledging and exploring them, you can align your actions with your well-being.

Self-Compassion Heals: Treating yourself with kindness and understanding, as highlighted by Dr. Kristin Neff, reduces self-criticism, fosters resilience, and supports emotional regulation.

The Inner Encourager Overpowers the Inner Critic: Amplify the voice of your Inner Encourager to strengthen your resilience, reframe challenges, and align with your long-term goals.

Permission to Be Human: As Dr. Tal Ben-Shahar emphasizes, accepting your humanity—including your imperfections and struggles—is key to emotional healing and personal growth.

ACT Provides a Path Forward: Acceptance and Commitment Therapy helps you embrace discomfort, commit to values-based actions, and build psychological flexibility, empowering you to navigate life's challenges with grace and purpose.

# Empathy and Self-Compassion Pulse Check

Reflecting on your journey with the RECOVERY Sunshine Assessment, take a moment to evaluate your current level of empathy and self-compassion and how they are supporting your recovery. Consider this a focused check-in on this essential ray of sunshine, offering insight into where you are and where you can nurture growth.

Ascribe
On a scale of 1–10, how well do you feel you embody empathy and self-compassion? Use these questions to guide your rating:
- How often do you offer yourself kindness and understanding during difficult moments?
- When faced with emotions like sadness or anger, do you allow yourself to feel them without judgment?
- Do you respond to your mistakes or setbacks with self-criticism or self-compassion?
- How often do you remind yourself that struggles are a natural part of the human experience?
- Do you actively listen to and validate your own emotions?

Describe
Reflect on why you gave yourself that score:
- What recent experiences have challenged your ability to practice self-compassion or empathy?
- How have you responded to your emotions or setbacks during those times?
- In what moments did you show yourself understanding or kindness?

- How has your relationship with your emotions evolved recently?

Prescribe
Identify one action you can take to deepen your empathy and self-compassion:
- What's one small way you can show yourself kindness today?
- How can you validate and process an emotion you've been avoiding?
- What practice can you incorporate to nurture your emotional well-being?

Actionable Inspirations
Here are practical ways to strengthen your self-compassion and empathy:
- Take 5 minutes to sit with a challenging emotion. Observe it without judgment and ask, "What is this feeling trying to tell me?"
- Write yourself a letter from your Inner Encourager, offering understanding and support for a recent struggle.
- Practice Kristin Neff's *self-compassion break*: Pause, acknowledge your struggle, and remind yourself, "This is part of being human."
- Reflect on a moment of kindness you offered someone else and consider how you can extend that same grace to yourself.
- Use mindfulness to notice and name your emotions, creating space to respond with self-compassion rather than reaction.

Sentence Completions
Deepen your self-awareness and empathy with these prompts:
- When I feel overwhelmed, I can nurture myself by...
- A moment I showed myself compassion was...
- To grow in empathy for myself, I will...
- My emotions guide me by...
- I know I'm practicing self-compassion when I...

Mantra for Empathy and Self-Compassion
"I meet my emotions with kindness and embrace my humanity with compassion."

Or create your own:
_____

A SPARK of HOPE

Your Humanity Is Your Superpower. Every emotion, every struggle, every setback—they're all part of what makes you beautifully human. By meeting yourself with empathy and self-compassion, you create a foundation of strength that no challenge can shake. This isn't about never stumbling; it's about rising each time with a deeper understanding of who you are and where you're headed. Give yourself the permission to be human. Remember, resilience isn't built in the absence of difficulty but in how you rise to meet it, one intentional step at a time.

CHAPTER 4: EMPATHY AND SELF-COMPASSION

What sparked your curiosity or caught your attention?
(Reflect on what you found interesting or intriguing.)

_____
_____
_____
_____
_____

What insights or ideas feel actionable or relevant to your life?
(Identify what you can apply or implement.)

_____
_____
_____
_____
_____

What resonated deeply or felt personally meaningful to you?
(Consider what moved or inspired you emotionally or intellectually.)

_____
_____
_____
_____
_____

RECOVERY

CHAPTER 5

Connection and Positive Relationships

Connection is the thread that weaves meaning into our lives. From the warmth of shared laughter to the quiet strength of a supportive friend, relationships shape who we are and who we aspire to be. They give us the courage to face challenges and the joy to savor life's victories. In the context of recovery, connection becomes even more vital—it offers belonging, accountability, and the strength to move away from addictive behaviors. The beauty of connection lies in its accessibility; it's built moment by moment, choice by choice, and conversation by conversation. In this chapter, we'll explore the transformative power of relationships and discover practical ways to cultivate bonds that inspire growth and resilience.

CONNECTION AND POSITIVE RELATIONSHIPS

> *"We are wired for connection. Connection gives purpose and meaning to our lives."* – Brené Brown

Human beings are inherently social creatures, wired to seek connection and belonging. From the moment we're born, our relationships shape who we are, providing safety, identity, and purpose. These bonds are not just emotionally fulfilling—they are essential for our mental, emotional, and even physical well-being. As we navigate the complexities of life, the quality of our relationships profoundly influences our ability to cope with challenges, manage stress, and pursue a life of meaning.

Connection goes beyond the surface of casual interactions. It's about creating deep, authentic relationships that ground us, inspire us, and remind us that we are not alone. These relationships buffer us against life's stressors, reduce feelings of isolation, and provide the emotional support necessary to overcome difficulties. In the context of recovery or breaking free from addictive behaviors, connection becomes a lifeline, offering a healthier, more fulfilling alternative to harmful coping mechanisms.

In this chapter, we'll delve into the science of connection, explore the transformative impact of positive relationships, and provide actionable steps to cultivate deeper bonds. Through small, intentional acts, meaningful conversations, and the practice of mutual support, you can create a network of relationships that uplift and empower you. Connection is not just a feel-good concept; it's a powerful tool for resilience, growth, and lasting well-being. Let's explore how to build and nurture these vital bonds.

The Vital Role of Connection and Belonging in Well-Being: A Buffer Against Addictive Behaviors

Connection and belonging are fundamental human needs, intricately tied to our psychological and physical well-being. From our first moments, relationships form the bedrock of our development, offering us safety, identity, and a sense of purpose. As adults, these bonds continue to shape how we navigate life's challenges and process emotions. When we feel deeply connected and know we belong, our resilience grows, and the pull toward harmful coping mechanisms—like addictive behaviors—diminishes.

Why Connection Matters for Well-Being
Psychological research highlights the profound effects of connection on health and happiness. Dr. John Cacioppo, a leading figure in social neuroscience, found that loneliness can be as harmful to our health as smoking 15 cigarettes a day or being obese. On the flip side, meaningful relationships act as a protective shield, buffering us against stress and reducing risks of anxiety, depression, and other mental health struggles.

Emotionally, connection brings validation, empathy, and support. When we feel seen and understood by others, it helps us process emotions, navigate life's challenges, and find hope, even in difficult times. Dr. Brené Brown, an expert on vulnerability, reminds us that connection is why we are here—it gives meaning and purpose to our lives. Feeling deeply connected reassures us that we're not alone, creating a foundation for strength and resilience.

The Danger of Isolation and Addictive Behaviors
When the need for connection is unmet, isolation and loneliness can creep in, amplifying emotional pain and vulnerability. These feelings often lead people to seek escape or numbness, and addictive behaviors may become the stand-in for meaningful connection. For example, Dr. Gabor Maté, an expert on addiction, explains that addiction is often rooted in unmet emotional needs and disconnection, with substances or compulsive habits filling the void left by a lack of belonging.

Studies show a clear link between social disconnection and higher rates of substance use and other compulsive behaviors. Without supportive relationships, addiction can thrive, pulling individuals further into cycles of shame and isolation. Breaking this cycle begins with connection—rebuilding bridges to others and to oneself.

Connection as a Protective Factor Against Addictive Behaviors
Connection offers powerful protection against addiction, both as a preventative measure and during recovery. Here's how:

- **Emotional Regulation**: Healthy relationships provide safe spaces to express and process emotions, reducing the urge to numb them with harmful coping mechanisms.

- **Accountability and Encouragement**: Supportive friends, family, or groups help individuals stay aligned with recovery goals, offering a hand during setbacks and celebrating progress.

- **Fostering Meaning and Purpose**: Relationships often provide a sense of purpose and remind us of our values, making addictive behaviors less tempting.

- **Modeling Healthy Behaviors**: Surrounding yourself with people who prioritize well-being can inspire and reinforce positive habits.

Belonging: A Deeper Sense of Connection
Belonging isn't just about surface-level relationships; it's the profound feeling of being accepted and valued for who you are. This deep-rooted sense of belonging creates emotional security, allowing you to grow and thrive.

In recovery, belonging becomes especially powerful. Dr. Johann Hari, author of *Lost Connections*, emphasizes that "the opposite of addiction isn't sobriety—it's connection." Support groups like Alcoholics Anonymous or even informal gatherings of trusted friends create a sense of community. These spaces allow people to share experiences, foster hope, and gain practical guidance. Knowing that others understand your journey not only provides comfort but also inspires the strength to move forward.

Practical Steps to Cultivate Connection and Belonging
1. **Reach Out Regularly**

    Connection begins with small, consistent actions. Send a quick text, call a friend, or schedule a coffee date. As Johann Hari points out in *Lost Connections*, nurturing relationships is about quality, not perfection. A simple "thinking of you" can create a ripple effect of warmth and connection.

2. **Join Supportive Communities**

    Whether it's a recovery group, book club, or volunteer organization, finding like-minded individuals helps build a sense of belonging. Dr. Brené Brown emphasizes that belonging is about being accepted as your authentic self, and communities can provide the safe spaces to foster that acceptance.

3. **Be Present**

    Practice active listening and engage fully in your conversations. As Dr. John Gottman, a renowned relationship researcher, highlights, emotional connection grows when we offer our undivided attention and respond with empathy.

4. **Express Gratitude**

    Show appreciation for the people in your life. A heartfelt thank-you can strengthen bonds and encourage deeper connections. Dr. Robert Emmons, a leading expert on gratitude, found that expressing appreciation not only enriches relationships but also boosts personal well-being.

5. **Seek Professional Support**
   Therapy or counseling can be invaluable, especially if vulnerability or trust feels challenging. A therapist can guide you in building and maintaining healthy relationships while navigating the complexities of recovery and connection.

Connection and Belonging: The Path to Wholeness
At the heart of recovery lies the rediscovery of who you are and how you connect with the world around you. As social neuroscience reminds us, humans are wired for connection. Cultivating meaningful relationships offers the emotional support and purpose needed to break free from harmful cycles.

Healing doesn't have to be a solo journey. Whether through the unwavering love of a close friend, the encouragement of a support group, or the understanding of a therapist, connection reminds you that you are not alone. You are seen, valued, and capable of building a life filled with joy, meaning, and authentic belonging. Let connection guide you toward the wholeness you deserve.

The Power of Positive Relationships: A Buffer Against Stress and Addictive Behaviors

Positive relationships are more than just a source of joy—they are a cornerstone of emotional resilience and well-being. The people we connect with shape our experiences, help us navigate challenges, and influence our choices in profound ways. Research consistently shows that nurturing healthy, supportive relationships not only reduces stress but also provides a buffer against harmful coping mechanisms, such as addictive behaviors.

How Positive Relationships Reduce Stress
Stress is an inevitable part of life, but the presence of positive relationships can transform how we experience and manage it. Social neuroscience highlights that strong connections activate the brain's reward system, releasing oxytocin—a hormone that naturally calms stress and fosters feelings of safety and trust. This biological response explains why we often feel lighter and more secure when we share a tough moment with someone who genuinely cares.

A kind word, a listening ear, or simply having someone there during challenging times can make all the difference. Positive relationships offer:

- **Emotional Validation**: Reassurance that your feelings are seen, understood, and accepted.

- **Problem-Solving Support**: Practical advice or fresh perspectives that make challenges feel manageable.

- **Perspective**: A way to see your struggles through someone else's lens, easing feelings of isolation or helplessness.

Social Support and Addictive Behaviors
When positive relationships are lacking, the void is often filled with stress, loneliness, or emotional pain—key drivers behind addictive behaviors. Without healthy ways to cope, substances or compulsive habits may seem like a quick fix.

On the flip side, strong social connections can act as a powerful shield against these tendencies by:

Providing Emotional Stability: Reducing the need to numb feelings through harmful behaviors.

Fostering Accountability: Supportive people help you stay aligned with your goals, offering encouragement during rough patches.

Creating Belonging: Feeling connected eases loneliness, a significant trigger for addiction.

Modeling Healthy Behaviors: Surrounding yourself with people who prioritize well-being reinforces positive habits and inspires change.

Real-Life Impact: Relationships in Recovery
In recovery, relationships are not just helpful—they're essential. Support groups provide spaces for shared experiences, empathy, and encouragement. They remind us that we're not alone and offer practical tools for navigating the journey to well-being.

Join Our Community: Ready for Recovery
At **Ready for Recovery**, we believe that no one should face recovery alone. Our **monthly support group** provides a safe, compassionate space to connect with others who understand your journey. Whether you're seeking encouragement, resources, or simply a place to share, our community is here for you.

Visit **www.readyforrecovery.life** or scan the QR code to learn more and join us in building a life of resilience and connection.

Additional Support Groups to Explore
If you're looking for other opportunities to connect, consider these well-established support groups:

- **Alcoholics Anonymous (AA)**: A global fellowship providing mutual support for those recovering from alcohol addiction.

- **SMART Recovery**: Offers science-based tools and support to overcome addictive behaviors.

- **Narcotics Anonymous (NA)**: Focused on helping those recovering from drug addiction.

- **Al-Anon/Alateen**: Support groups for friends and family members of individuals struggling with addiction.

- **Celebrate Recovery**: A faith-based program addressing a wide range of life struggles, including addiction.

While these groups can provide invaluable support, **Ready for Recovery** is designed to foster connection and growth in a way that's unique to our shared mission. Together, we empower each other to overcome challenges and create lives aligned with our values.

Building and Strengthening Positive Relationships
Creating positive relationships takes intention and effort. Here are some steps to build and nurture those bonds:

- **Focus on Depth Over Breadth**: Prioritize a few meaningful relationships rather than spreading yourself too thin.

- **Practice Active Listening**: Listen without judgment and respond with empathy to build authentic connections.

- **Be Open and Vulnerable**: Sharing your thoughts and feelings builds trust and deepens relationships.

- **Show Gratitude**: Regularly express appreciation for those in your life. A simple "thank you" can go a long way.

- **Set Healthy Boundaries**: Relationships should be mutual and supportive. Avoid dynamics that add stress or negativity.

Connection as a Tool for Resilience
Positive relationships not only reduce stress but also boost resilience—the ability to face adversity and bounce back stronger. Knowing that you have people who care about your well-being can be the anchor you need to weather life's storms.

Connection: A Lifeline to Well-Being
Relationships are at the core of what it means to be human. They provide emotional nourishment, support, and purpose, especially for those navigating recovery or seeking to avoid harmful patterns.

Reaching out is not a sign of weakness—it's a courageous investment in your well-being. Whether you're leaning on a friend, joining a group, or simply spending quality time with loved ones, every effort strengthens the foundation that keeps you grounded, resilient, and thriving.

As Brené Brown reminds us, "We are hardwired for connection, and it is what gives purpose and meaning to our lives." By prioritizing relationships, you're not just healing—you're building a life worth celebrating.

The Science of Connection: How Social Interactions Boost Well-Being and Help With Addictive Behaviors

As Dr. Chris Peterson, one of the founding figures in positive psychology, famously put it: "Other people matter." This simple yet profound truth reminds us that human connection is at the heart of well-being. Relationships not only shape our emotional lives but also profoundly influence our biology.

Positive social interactions activate the brain's reward pathways and release **oxytocin**, sometimes called the "bonding hormone." This incredible neurochemical creates feelings of trust, safety, and belonging while reducing stress. It's no wonder connection is such a powerful ally in overcoming addictive behaviors.

What Is Oxytocin and Why Does It Matter?

Think of oxytocin as your brain's way of giving you a hug from the inside. It's released during positive interactions like hugging, sharing meaningful conversations, or even locking eyes with someone. This hormone strengthens trust and emotional bonds, all while calming your nervous system. According to researchers like Dr. Sue Carter, oxytocin even helps lower cortisol levels, your body's primary stress hormone. This combination of reduced stress and enhanced connection helps you feel emotionally safe and resilient.

How Social Interactions Reward the Brain

Did you know that spending time with someone you care about activates the same reward pathways in your brain as other pleasurable activities? That's because connection triggers the release of **dopamine**, the "feel-good" neurotransmitter that reinforces positive behavior.

This overlap is significant for recovery. Addictive behaviors also hijack these pathways, but healthy social bonding provides a natural—and far more sustainable—source of pleasure and motivation. Instead of numbing pain or stress, meaningful interactions help you engage with life in a fulfilling way.

The Role of Connection in Recovery

When you're navigating recovery, connection is like having an emotional safety net. Addiction often thrives in isolation, but relationships offer a counterbalance—fulfilling your need for belonging while easing feelings of loneliness. Whether it's through family, friends, or a supportive group like **Ready for Recovery**, meaningful connections help:

Provide Emotional Support: There's nothing quite like feeling understood. A network of supportive people can ease the emotional weight of recovery.

- **Offer Accountability**: Loved ones and peers can help you stay on track with your recovery goals and cheer you on through every small victory.

- **Share Experiences**: Knowing others are walking a similar path fosters hope and reminds you that you're never alone in your struggles.

- **Reduce Stress Naturally**: Positive interactions boost oxytocin and reduce cortisol, making it easier to manage life's challenges.

Why Connection Is So Powerful
As Dr. Chris Peterson so succinctly said, "Other people matter." When we invest in relationships, we activate the natural systems in our brains that promote trust, calm, and motivation. As Dr. Sue Carter and others have highlighted, oxytocin and dopamine work together to create a sense of belonging and emotional safety. These systems, activated through social bonding, counteract the pull of addictive behaviors by offering a healthier and more sustainable source of relief and reward.

Building Connection: How to Strengthen Social Bonds
Connection and belonging are essential to a fulfilling life, forming the foundation for resilience, emotional well-being, and growth. Whether you're looking to deepen relationships, reduce stress, or foster a sense of purpose, building meaningful bonds with others is a powerful way to enrich your life. Here are practical and research-backed strategies to strengthen social bonds:

- **Practice Active Constructive Listening**
  Engage fully in conversations by responding with genuine enthusiasm and curiosity when others share their experiences. Dr. Shelly Gable's research highlights how active constructive responses strengthen relationships and boost well-being. For instance, when a friend shares an accomplishment, rather than a simple "That's nice," try: "That's fantastic! I'm so proud of you—how did you make it happen?"

- **Prioritize Quality Time**
  Be intentional about spending meaningful time with loved ones. Shared activities like cooking together, taking a nature walk, or having a game night foster deeper emotional bonds. As Dr. Brené Brown emphasizes, connection flourishes in moments of shared presence.

- **Be Vulnerable and Share Authentically**
  Building trust involves letting others see the real you. Share your feelings, thoughts, and experiences with trusted individuals. Vulnerability invites authenticity from others, creating reciprocal emotional connections.

- **Express Gratitude and Appreciation**
  A simple "I appreciate you" or "Thanks for always having my back" goes a long way. Regularly acknowledging the people in your life strengthens bonds and reinforces mutual care. Positive psychology research shows that expressing gratitude enhances relationship satisfaction and emotional closeness.

- **Engage in Collaborative Activities**
  Working on a project together—like gardening, cooking, or assembling furniture—creates shared goals and strengthens connection through teamwork. Think of it as building something tangible while deepening your relationship.

- **Reach Out Regularly**
  Consistency matters. Even a quick "Thinking of you" text or a five-minute phone call keeps the connection alive. Relationships, like plants, thrive when nurtured regularly.

- **Show Up for Important Moments**
  Celebrating milestones, attending events, or simply being there when it matters most signals care and commitment. Research by Dr. John Gottman suggests that showing up during key moments strengthens emotional trust.

- **Participate in Playful Activities**
  Laughter is a universal connector. Try lighthearted activities like board games, outdoor sports, or even a TikTok dance challenge to inject joy and build bonds. Dr. Stuart Brown's work on play shows that it fosters creativity, trust, and emotional connection.

- **Create Rituals of Connection**
  Rituals create consistent opportunities for bonding. Whether it's a weekly brunch with friends, a nightly phone call with a family member, or an annual getaway, these habits cultivate connection and belonging.

- **Offer Help and Support**
  Acts of kindness—big or small—strengthen trust and show care. Helping someone move, watching a friend's kids, or lending a listening ear demonstrates that you value the relationship.

Why These Practices Matter
By engaging in these intentional practices, you create opportunities for meaningful, lasting connections that enrich your life. Connection isn't about how many people you know but about the depth and quality of your relationships. Strong bonds not only enhance well-being but also act as a protective buffer against stress and the pull of harmful behaviors.

As Dr. John M. Gottman, famously said, "Successful long-term relationships are created through small words, small gestures, and small acts." These small, consistent actions remind us that connection is at the heart of a flourishing life.

The Role of Connection in Preventing Addictive Behaviors
Connection is both a source of emotional nourishment and a natural reward system for the brain. It fulfills the human need for bonding and belonging, reducing the appeal of unhealthy substitutes like addictive behaviors. By offering emotional

fulfillment and activating oxytocin and dopamine, relationships create a protective barrier against isolation and stress.

Why Positive Relationships Matter in Recovery and Beyond

Positive relationships are not just about proximity—they are about depth, mutual care, and authenticity. These relationships provide:

- **Empathy and Support**: Spaces for understanding and encouragement during challenges.

- **Boundaries and Balance**: Respect for individual needs and limits.

- **Mutual Growth**: Motivation to pursue personal and collective well-being.

For those in recovery, connection is transformative. It offers accountability, fosters resilience, and reminds you that you are not alone. Building and maintaining positive relationships can break cycles of isolation and create a foundation for lasting well-being.

The Power of Connection, Accountability, and Role Models: Choosing Your Circle for Positive Change

Who we spend time with shapes who we become. This truth is particularly relevant when it comes to preventing addictive

CHAPTER 5: CONNECTION AND POSITIVE RELATIONSHIPS

behaviors and fostering a life of well-being and purpose. Connection, accountability, and role models are critical elements in creating an environment that supports positive choices and personal growth. By surrounding yourself with the right people, you can build a network that inspires resilience, reinforces your goals, and strengthens your ability to navigate challenges.

When you are surrounded by caring and supportive individuals, you are less likely to seek solace in harmful behaviors.

Key ways to build supportive connections include:
Spending time with people who uplift you: Prioritize relationships that encourage growth and well-being.

Engaging in shared activities: Whether it's exercising, cooking, or simply talking, shared experiences strengthen bonds.

Reaching out during tough times: Vulnerability fosters deeper connections and ensures you don't face challenges alone.

Accountability: Staying True to Your Goals
Accountability is the glue that holds commitments together. Having someone to check in with regularly—whether a friend, coach, or mentor—keeps you aligned with your goals and reminds you of your progress. In preventing addictive behaviors, accountability partners can provide the motivation and perspective needed to stay on track.

Ways accountability supports positive behavior:
Regular check-ins: Set up a schedule to discuss your goals and challenges with a trusted individual.

Mutual encouragement: Accountability is a two-way street; supporting others can also reinforce your own commitment.

Tracking progress: Sharing milestones and setbacks with someone helps build resilience and keeps you focused on your long-term vision.

Role Models: Inspiring Positive Change
Role models play a pivotal role in shaping behavior and mindset. Observing and learning from individuals who embody the values and lifestyle you aspire to can provide both inspiration and a roadmap for success. Role models demonstrate that change is possible and offer practical insights on how to navigate challenges.

When choosing role models, look for:
People who live with integrity: Surround yourself with individuals who align their actions with their values.

Those who have overcome adversity: Learning from people who have faced and triumphed over similar struggles can be deeply motivating.

Positive influencers in your life: This could be a family member, a colleague, or even a public figure whose journey resonates with you.

Choosing Your Circle: Why It Matters
The people you spend the most time with influence your habits, thoughts, and decisions. A supportive, goal-oriented social circle can act as a buffer against stress and temptation, while

a toxic environment can reinforce unhealthy patterns. As Jim Rohn famously said, "You are the average of the five people you spend the most time with."

To cultivate a positive circle:
Evaluate your relationships: Reflect on who supports and inspires you, and who may be pulling you away from your goals.

Seek out growth-oriented communities: Join groups or organizations that align with your values and interests.

Be intentional: Choose to invest in relationships that foster accountability, growth, and positivity.

The Ripple Effect of Connection
When you surround yourself with supportive, inspiring individuals, their influence ripples into your choices, habits, and outlook on life. Connection, accountability, and role models are not just tools for preventing addictive behaviors—they are the foundation for a thriving and fulfilling life.

Remember, the people in your circle shape your trajectory. By intentionally choosing connection, fostering accountability, and seeking role models who align with your values, you create an environment where positive change becomes inevitable. Let your circle empower you to become the best version of yourself.

Positive relationships are a cornerstone of recovery, offering encouragement, healthy modeling, and a sense of shared purpose. They help rebuild confidence by celebrating progress and reframing setbacks as learning opportunities. Watching others navigate challenges provides practical insights into healthier coping mechanisms, as emphasized by social learning theory (Bandura, 1977). Moreover, relationships that foster a shared purpose remind us that recovery is not just about personal healing—it connects us to something greater, reinforcing motivation and resilience.

Micro Moments of Connection: The Small Interactions That Matter

In the hustle of daily life, it's easy to underestimate the power of small interactions—those fleeting moments that can brighten a day, deepen a relationship, or even elevate your overall well-being. These "micro moments" of connection might seem insignificant, but they hold immense potential to create trust, joy, and a profound sense of belonging. Dr. Barbara Fredrickson, a leading voice in positive psychology, refers to these shared experiences as *positivity resonance*—moments where emotional connection is mutual and transformative.

What Are Micro Moments of Connection?
Micro moments of connection are brief but impactful interactions—like a warm smile exchanged with a stranger, a heartfelt thank you to a barista, or a quick but meaningful chat with a loved one. These moments are powerful because they activate the brain's reward system, releasing oxytocin, often called the "bonding hormone" (Carter, 2014). This chemical boost not only enhances trust but also reduces stress, creating an immediate sense of calm and connection.

Why Micro Moments Matter
Though small in scale, micro moments are transformative. They remind us that we're part of a larger human experience, reducing feelings of isolation and strengthening empathy. When you share one of these moments, it's not just your well-being that benefits—research by Fredrickson (2013) suggests that positivity resonance amplifies the emotional connection for both parties, creating a ripple effect of kindness and understanding.

These interactions also:
- **Lower Stress**: By reducing cortisol levels and calming the nervous system.

- **Foster Belonging**: Reinforcing that you are seen, valued, and part of a community.

- **Build Empathy**: Encouraging mutual care and understanding through shared experiences.

▶ **Try This: Micro-Moments of Connection Exercise**

Fostering these connections doesn't require grand gestures—just presence and intention. Here's how you can cultivate micro moments in everyday life:

- **Be Present**: Set aside distractions like your phone and give the other person your full attention, even during brief exchanges.

- **Offer Genuine Compliments**: A simple, "You did a great job on that," can create a meaningful connection.

- **Use Names**: Addressing someone by their name adds a personal touch and fosters a sense of significance.

- **Express Gratitude**: Whether it's thanking a coworker or acknowledging a kind gesture, heartfelt appreciation strengthens bonds.

- **Practice Active Listening**: Even in a short interaction, making someone feel heard can leave a lasting impact.

- **Fostering Connection Through Curiosity:** Coined by Edgar Schein, **humble inquiry** is the art of asking open, thoughtful questions that invite genuine connection. This approach nurtures trust and deepens relationships by prioritizing curiosity over judgment, creating a safe space for honest sharing. By simply asking, "What was that experience like for you?" or "How can I support you?" you show genuine interest, fostering a sense of value and belonging. Practicing humble inquiry transforms micro-moments into profound opportunities for connection, enhancing mutual understanding and emotional resonance.

The Science of Small Connections
Fredrickson's research highlights that positivity resonance—the emotional uplift from shared positive interactions—builds cumulatively. Each micro moment strengthens emotional and psychological well-being, reinforcing that even small connections carry immense weight. Over time, these brief exchanges

can create a network of emotional safety and positivity that enriches both individual lives and communities.

A Daily Practice
Micro moments are accessible to everyone, every day. Challenge yourself to:

- Smile at a passerby.
- Hold the door for someone and exchange a kind word.
- Compliment a colleague on their effort.
- Thank someone who often goes unnoticed, like a delivery driver or teacher.
- Share a quick laugh with a friend or loved one.

These small acts ripple outward, inspiring further connections and reminding us of the shared beauty in being human.

Why It Matters
As Dr. Fredrickson emphasizes, *positivity resonance* helps us experience the best in ourselves and others. Micro moments of connection might seem trivial, but they are the threads that weave the fabric of our well-being. By creating these moments, you're not only nurturing your own sense of joy and purpose but also uplifting the people around you.

So, pause and notice the opportunities for connection all around you. A simple smile or kind word might be exactly what someone—and you—need today.

Acts of Connection: Strengthening Bonds and Supporting Recovery

Connection doesn't happen by chance—it thrives through intentional actions that foster trust, belonging, and mutual respect. Acts of connection are deliberate efforts to show others they are valued and cared for, creating a ripple effect of kindness that strengthens relationships and emotional well-being.

Why Acts of Connection Matter
Even the simplest gestures can profoundly impact both the giver and the receiver:

- **Reinforce Relationships:** Regular, thoughtful actions help keep bonds strong.

- **Combat Isolation:** Connection reduces loneliness and creates a sense of belonging.

- **Support Recovery:** In moments of struggle, these acts remind us of the support system we have and reduce the pull toward addictive behaviors.

- **Boost Emotional Health:** Small acts of kindness can release oxytocin, promoting trust and reducing stress.

Simple Yet Powerful Ideas
- **Check-In Calls or Texts:** A quick, "How are you doing?" can mean the world to someone.

- **Celebrate Milestones:** Acknowledge birthdays, anniversaries, or personal achievements to show you care.

- **Small Acts of Kindness:** Share a meal, bring coffee, or offer to help with a task—these gestures build trust and appreciation.

- **Be Fully Present:** Sometimes, the most impactful gift is your undivided attention.

Creating a Habit of Connection

- **Be Intentional:** Plan acts of connection into your daily routine.

- **Look for Opportunities:** Notice when someone could use encouragement or support.

- **Practice Gratitude:** Acknowledge the people who uplift and inspire you.

How Acts of Connection Support Recovery
In the context of recovery or overcoming addictive behaviors, these acts provide more than emotional support—they create accountability, promote resilience, and fulfill the need for bonding that addictive behaviors often replace. Small but meaningful interactions serve as a reminder that you are not alone and that healthy, positive connections can be a powerful alternative to harmful coping mechanisms.

By integrating acts of connection with practices like humble inquiry and micro moments, you can cultivate deeper relationships that foster growth, joy, and well-being. These intentional actions ground us in a sense of shared humanity, reminding us that connection is not only vital for relationships but also for personal transformation.

Chapter Summary

Connection and positive relationships are the foundation of resilience and well-being. They reduce isolation, provide emotional support, and foster accountability, creating a strong buffer against life's challenges, including addictive behaviors. By embracing intentional acts of connection—like micro moments of kindness and meaningful conversations—you can nurture bonds that inspire growth and healing.

Positive relationships ground you in shared purpose, remind you of your worth, and align you with your values. Each small interaction strengthens your ability to navigate challenges, reinforcing that connection isn't just support—it's a pathway to a fulfilling, purpose-driven life. Choose to invest in these connections and let them guide you toward joy and lasting well-being.

Key Takeaways

Connection Fuels Resilience: Positive relationships buffer against stress, promote emotional regulation, and reduce the appeal of addictive behaviors by fulfilling the brain's natural need for bonding.

The Power of Small Gestures: Micro moments of connection—smiles, kind words, and active listening—activate the brain's reward pathways, fostering trust and reducing stress.

Humble Inquiry Deepens Bonds: By asking open-ended questions and listening with genuine curiosity, you create a safe space for deeper emotional connection and trust.

Acts of Connection Matter: Intentional gestures, from check-in texts to shared activities, reinforce relationships, reduce loneliness, and promote mutual support.

Positive Relationships Shape Growth: Surrounding yourself with supportive, growth-oriented individuals helps you adopt healthier coping strategies, stay accountable to your goals, and build confidence.

Belonging Is Transformative: A sense of belonging, whether through close friendships, support groups, or family bonds, fosters purpose and resilience, anchoring you in a community of mutual care.

Choose Your Circle Wisely: The people you surround yourself with influence your habits, thoughts, and well-being. Prioritize relationships that align with your values and inspire your growth.

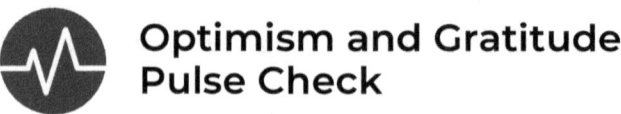
Optimism and Gratitude Pulse Check

Reflecting on your journey with the RECOVERY Sunshine Assessment, take a moment to evaluate your current level of optimism and gratitude and how they are shaping your well-being and recovery. Consider this a focused check-in on this essential ray of sunshine, offering insight into where you are and where you can cultivate growth.

Ascribe

On a scale of 1–10, how present are optimism and gratitude in your daily life? Use these questions to guide your rating:
- How often do you find yourself focusing on what's possible rather than what's wrong?
- Do you regularly acknowledge the things you're grateful for, even amidst challenges?
- When faced with setbacks, do you believe they are temporary and surmountable?
- How often do you reframe difficult situations with a sense of hope or possibility?
- Do you notice and appreciate small joys or moments of connection throughout your day?

Describe

Reflect on why you gave yourself that score:
- What recent experiences have influenced your ability to practice gratitude and optimism?
- Have you noticed patterns of negative thinking, or have you been able to reframe challenges constructively?

- What moments stand out where you felt particularly hopeful or grateful?
- In what ways have gratitude or optimism helped you navigate a tough situation?

Prescribe
Identify one action you can take to enhance your practice of optimism and gratitude:
- What's one small thing you can do today to express gratitude for someone or something in your life?
- How can you reframe a current challenge to focus on opportunities rather than obstacles?
- What's one positive outcome you can visualize for yourself this week?

Actionable Inspirations
Here are practical ways to strengthen your optimism and gratitude practices:
- Write down three things you're grateful for each day, focusing on small, specific moments.
- Reframe a negative thought by asking, "What's one thing I can learn or gain from this situation?"
- Create a gratitude ritual, like pausing before meals to reflect on something you appreciate.
- Start your day by visualizing one positive outcome or goal you want to work toward.
- Share your gratitude with others through a note, text, or meaningful conversation.

Sentence Completions
Deepen your optimism and gratitude practice with these prompts:
- A moment I felt truly hopeful was…
- Today, I am grateful for…
- To cultivate optimism, I will…
- A small joy I noticed recently was…
- I can reframe this challenge by…

Mantra for Optimism and Gratitude
"I embrace hope and gratitude, finding strength and joy in each moment."

Or create your own:
_____

A SPARK of HOPE

Every moment is an opportunity to connect—whether through a kind word, a listening ear, or a simple gesture of presence. As you lean into building these bonds, remember that connection is a two-way street. Just as others uplift and inspire you, your actions and presence can create ripples of positivity in their lives. Trust in the power of small, intentional moments to strengthen your relationships and enrich your recovery journey. You don't have to walk this path alone; let the connections you foster remind you that together, we are stronger, braver, and infinitely more resilient.

CHAPTER 5: CONNECTION AND POSITIVE RELATIONSHIPS

What sparked your curiosity or caught your attention?
(Reflect on what you found interesting or intriguing.)

_____
_____
_____
_____
_____

What insights or ideas feel actionable or relevant to your life?
(Identify what you can apply or implement.)

_____
_____
_____
_____
_____

What resonated deeply or felt personally meaningful to you?
(Consider what moved or inspired you emotionally or intellectually.)

_____
_____
_____
_____
_____

CHAPTER 6

Optimism and Gratitude

What you focus on grows. Optimism and gratitude are more than just feel-good practices; they are transformative tools that invite us to reframe challenges, embrace possibilities, and find strength even in our darkest moments. They aren't about glossing over pain or forcing positivity but about recognizing the resilience within us and choosing to focus on what uplifts and inspires us. When paired with the courage to face struggles head-on, these practices become the foundation for hope—a vital force that fuels recovery and opens the door to profound growth.

OPTIMISM AND GRATITUDE

***"The more grateful I am,
the more beauty I see"*** – Mary Davis

In the journey of recovery, optimism and gratitude are not just comforting ideas—they are transformative tools that reshape how we see ourselves, our challenges, and our possibilities. Rooted in positive psychology and supported by compelling research, these practices form a foundation for resilience and well-being.

Optimism empowers you to view setbacks not as permanent roadblocks but as opportunities for growth and learning. It's not about denying hardship but about choosing to focus on potential solutions and brighter possibilities. Gratitude, on the other hand, centers your attention on the moments of connection, support, and progress that often go unnoticed, helping you find meaning even in the midst of struggle. Together, they counteract negative thought patterns, reduce emotional burdens, and bring clarity and hope to your recovery journey.

This chapter invites you to explore the profound impact of optimism and gratitude. Through practical strategies and research-backed insights, you'll discover how these practices can reframe challenges, foster emotional resilience, and guide you toward a life grounded in balance, growth, and fulfillment. Whether it's finding hope in difficult moments or celebrating the small wins along the way, optimism and gratitude are your companions on the path to recovery.

Authentic Optimism and Gratitude: Tools for Resilience and Recovery

In a world full of positivity mantras and quick-fix motivational soundbites, it's easy to misunderstand optimism and gratitude as shallow or dismissive concepts. However, true optimism and gratitude are rooted in emotional honesty and resilience, offering a grounded way to engage with life's complexities. Unlike toxic positivity, which dismisses challenges with phrases like, "Just be happy," these practices embrace the full range of human emotions, providing space for both joy and pain.

Not About Avoidance or Denial
Optimism and gratitude do not ask you to ignore hardship or push away difficult emotions. Instead, they encourage you to face challenges head-on with a perspective that fosters growth and healing:

- **Optimism** allows you to acknowledge obstacles while focusing on possibilities, saying, "This is hard, but I can find a way through."

- **Gratitude** helps you ground yourself in the present, appreciating the support, strength, or resources that coexist with your struggles.

These practices invite engagement with reality, offering tools to navigate difficulties rather than avoid them.

Fostering Resilience, Not Avoidance
Optimism and gratitude strengthen resilience by shifting focus from what's wrong to what's possible or meaningful. They encourage you to reframe setbacks as opportunities for growth while honoring the emotions that arise along the way.

- **Optimism** fuels hope and motivation, making it easier to take constructive action even in tough times.

- **Gratitude** creates moments of calm and connection, helping you appreciate the support and resources that sustain you.

How This Helps With Addictive Behaviors
For those struggling with addictive behaviors, optimism and gratitude can be transformative. Addiction often thrives on feelings of hopelessness, disconnection, or a desire to numb emotional pain. By fostering emotional resilience and a sense of connection, these practices help counteract those tendencies:

- **Optimism** provides hope for a better future, inspiring small but meaningful steps toward recovery.

- **Gratitude** shifts focus to what is supportive and meaningful, reducing the emotional pull toward unhealthy coping mechanisms.

Beyond Happyology: The Truth About Gratitude

Gratitude isn't about forcing happiness or pretending everything is fine. Unlike toxic positivity, which dismisses valid emotions, gratitude welcomes the complexity of life. It allows you to say, "This is hard, but I'm thankful for what helps me endure," rather than denying your struggles.

For example, instead of dismissing a tough workday with "Just be happy you have a job," a gratitude-centered approach might be, "Work has been overwhelming, but I'm grateful for my supportive colleagues." This balanced perspective validates the challenge while fostering connection and resilience.

Optimism and gratitude are not about avoiding life's difficulties but about finding strength and meaning within them. They empower you to confront challenges with courage, offering tools to move beyond addictive behaviors and build a life rooted in hope, growth, and emotional authenticity.

Understanding the Negativity Bias and Automatic Negative Thoughts: How Gratitude and Optimism Transform Recovery
Our brains are naturally wired to focus on the negative—a tendency known as the negativity bias. While this evolutionary survival mechanism helped our ancestors stay alert to danger, it often works against us in modern life, amplifying setbacks and making it harder to notice the good. For those navigating recovery from addictive behaviors, this bias can magnify slip-ups, leading to feelings of failure and hopelessness.

Compounding this is the presence of Automatic Negative Thoughts (ANTs)—those reflexive, self-critical voices that creep in during moments of stress or uncertainty. Phrases like *"I'll never get this right"* or *"I'm not strong enough to change"* are common examples that can erode confidence and fuel harmful habits.

Why the Negativity Bias and ANTs Matter in Recovery

The negativity bias ensures that negative experiences leave a stronger emotional imprint than positive ones, often overshadowing progress. For example:

- A single slip in sobriety may feel more significant than weeks of success.

- One argument with a loved one can feel like proof that relationships aren't working.

- A fleeting doubt may seem like evidence that change is impossible.

ANTs add to this challenge by reinforcing negative self-beliefs. Thoughts like *"I've ruined everything"* or *"I'll never overcome this"* can become triggers for returning to addictive behaviors as a way to escape the spiral of shame or frustration.

The Role of Gratitude and Optimism
Gratitude and optimism are powerful tools to counteract these mental traps, helping rewire the brain toward a more constructive outlook. Unlike toxic positivity, which dismisses pain,

these practices embrace emotional honesty while providing a path forward.

How Gratitude Helps
Gratitude activates the brain's reward system, releasing dopamine and reinforcing positive thought patterns. Dr. Robert Emmons, a leading expert on gratitude, explains that regular gratitude practices strengthen neural pathways, making it easier to focus on what's going well. This shift reduces the emotional weight of negative experiences and fosters resilience.

How Optimism Helps
Optimism builds hope and emotional regulation by framing challenges as opportunities for growth. Studies show that optimistic individuals recover from stress more quickly and are better equipped to handle setbacks. In recovery, optimism acts as a compass, guiding you toward a better future and reminding you that change is possible.

Practical Strategies to Overcome Negativity Bias and ANTs
1. **Gratitude Journaling**
   Spend a few minutes each day writing down three things you're grateful for. Focus on specific moments, such as a supportive conversation or progress you've made.

2. **Reframe Negative Thoughts**
   When an ANT arises, challenge it:
   - Ask yourself, *"Is this thought factual or just an assumption?"*

- Replace it with a hopeful statement. For example, instead of *"I'll never succeed,"* try, *"I'm making progress one step at a time."*

3. **Mindful Gratitude**
   Incorporate gratitude into mindfulness practices. Pay attention to simple, present-moment experiences—a warm drink, the sound of nature, or the kindness of a friend.

4. **Visualize Positive Outcomes**
   Each morning, visualize one positive action you want to take that day. This primes your brain for optimism and sets a constructive tone.

How These Practices Support Recovery

Gratitude and optimism provide emotional tools that help manage stress and reduce the pull of addictive behaviors. While the negativity bias and ANTs may be natural tendencies, they don't have to dictate your experience. By integrating gratitude and optimism into your daily life, you create a balanced perspective—one that honors the challenges while celebrating the progress. These practices build resilience, foster emotional growth, and help you align with healthier, more fulfilling behaviors.

Recovery isn't about avoiding life's difficulties but about meeting them with hope, gratitude, and determination. Each moment is a chance to rewrite the narrative—one thought, one action, one day at a time.

Cognitive Distortions: Understanding and Overcoming Mental Traps

Our minds are powerful, but they can sometimes mislead us. Cognitive distortions—habitual, biased patterns of thinking—can warp how we perceive ourselves and our challenges, particularly in moments of stress or uncertainty. These mental traps often fuel addictive behaviors, acting as barriers to well-being and recovery.

The good news? With awareness and tools like gratitude and optimism, you can challenge these distortions and create a healthier, more constructive mindset.

Common Cognitive Distortions and Their Role in Addictive Behaviors
Here are the most common cognitive distortions that tend to play a role in the cycle of addictive behaviors:

- **All-or-Nothing Thinking:** Viewing situations in extremes, with no middle ground.
  Example: "I had one drink, so I might as well keep going—I've already failed."
  This type of thinking often leads to abandoning efforts after minor setbacks, making recovery feel like an all-or-nothing game.

- **Catastrophizing:** Expecting the worst possible outcome.
  Example: "If I don't use, I won't be able to handle the stress, and everything will fall apart."

This distortion magnifies challenges and makes addictive behaviors seem like the only viable coping mechanism.

- **Negative Filtering:** Focusing exclusively on the bad while ignoring the good.
  Example: "Even though I've been sober for weeks, one bad day proves I'm not making progress."
  This distortion minimizes hard-earned wins and reinforces feelings of failure or hopelessness.

- **Emotional Reasoning:** Believing that emotions reflect reality.
  Example: "I feel like I can't cope, so I must be incapable of recovery."
  This distortion ties temporary feelings to fixed conclusions, discouraging constructive action.

- **Personalization:** Blaming yourself for things outside your control.
  Example: "It's my fault my relationships have fallen apart—I ruin everything."
  This type of thinking amplifies guilt and shame, common triggers for addictive behaviors.

How Gratitude and Optimism Counter Cognitive Distortions

Gratitude and optimism act as powerful antidotes to these mental traps, helping you challenge distorted thoughts and create space for healthier, more balanced perspectives.

- **Gratitude** shifts focus from what's going wrong to what's going right, countering distortions like negative filtering or disqualifying the positive.
  Example: Instead of dwelling on a slip-up, gratitude helps you recognize your progress: "I had one bad day, but I've had many good ones, and I'm capable of continuing."

- **Optimism** reframes catastrophic thinking into hope for better outcomes.
  Example: Replace, "I'll never get this right," with, "I'm learning from every step, and progress takes time."

- Both practices encourage self-compassion, helping you respond to personalization or emotional reasoning with kindness and curiosity rather than self-criticism.

▶ **Try This: Challenge Cognitive Distortions Exercise**

Here are ways to identify and overcome distorted thinking:

- **Spot the Distortion:** When a negative thought arises, pause and ask yourself, *"Is this thought true, or is it my inner critic talking?"*

- **Reframe with Optimism:** Shift from a fixed mindset to a growth mindset.
  Example: "I'll never succeed" becomes, "I'm learning and growing, even when it's hard."

- **Focus on Gratitude:** Counter negative filtering by listing three things going well, even on difficult days.

- **Reality-Check Your Emotions:** When you catch yourself in emotional reasoning, remind yourself, "Just because I feel this way doesn't mean it's true."

- **Celebrate Small Wins:** Give equal weight to small victories, such as resisting temptation or reaching out for support.

Why This Matters in Recovery
Cognitive distortions can keep you trapped in the cycle of addictive behaviors by reinforcing feelings of failure, shame, and hopelessness. Gratitude and optimism help break this cycle by shifting your focus toward possibilities and progress. They create a mental framework that supports resilience, empowers constructive choices, and reduces the emotional pull of harmful habits.

For example:
- Gratitude helps you acknowledge the support and tools available, even during setbacks.

- Optimism reminds you that every day is an opportunity to grow, no matter how many times you've struggled.

A Balanced Mindset for Recovery
Cognitive distortions may be hardwired into the brain, but they are not set in stone. By practicing gratitude and optimism, you can challenge these patterns, rewire your thinking, and foster a

mindset that supports recovery. Remember, overcoming distorted thoughts is not about denying difficulties but about choosing to see the whole picture—one that includes both challenges and the possibility for growth.

Your thoughts are powerful allies when you learn to guide them. Recovery isn't about perfect thinking; it's about developing the resilience to question unhelpful patterns and choose perspectives that strengthen your journey.

The Power of Optimism: Reframing Challenges with Hope

Optimism isn't just about looking on the bright side—it's a practical mindset that helps you face life's hurdles with resilience and determination. At its heart, optimism is the belief that setbacks are temporary, difficulties can be overcome, and the future holds promise. It's like having a trusted guide reminding you, *"This won't last forever, and you've got what it takes to move forward."* This perspective doesn't erase challenges but helps you approach them with strength and curiosity.

When paired with hope, optimism becomes a powerful tool for reframing challenges, turning roadblocks into stepping stones. This mindset fosters the determination to adapt, persevere, and ultimately thrive.

The Science Behind Optimism
Psychological research backs up the transformative power of optimism. Dr. Martin Seligman, a pioneer in positive psychology,

notes that optimistic people tend to view challenges as specific, temporary, and external rather than pervasive, permanent, and personal. For instance, instead of thinking, *"I always mess up,"* an optimist might say, *"This mistake was just one moment—it doesn't define me."* This shift in thinking promotes emotional resilience and helps you bounce back from adversity.

Optimism also affects the brain at a biological level. When you anticipate positive outcomes, your brain releases dopamine, a neurotransmitter tied to motivation and pleasure. This process reinforces hopeful thinking and encourages proactive behavior. In other words, optimism doesn't just help you think better—it motivates you to *act* better.

Reframing Challenges with Hope
Life's difficulties are unavoidable, but optimism provides the tools to approach them with confidence and creativity. Here's how you can reframe challenges with hope:

- **Focus on What You Can Control:**
  Feeling overwhelmed? Shift your focus to small, actionable steps you can take. For example, if you're navigating recovery, instead of fixating on how long the journey might be, focus on what you can do *today* to move closer to your goal.

- **Look for the Lesson:**
  Challenges often come with hidden opportunities for growth. Ask yourself, *"What is this situation teaching me?"* By viewing setbacks as learning experiences, you turn difficulties into stepping stones.

- **Visualize Positive Outcomes:**
  Imagine yourself on the other side of the challenge, having navigated it successfully. This practice helps keep your focus on possibilities rather than problems, giving you the energy to push forward.

- **Shift the Narrative:**
  Language shapes perception. Instead of saying, *"This is impossible,"* try, *"This is tough, but I can handle it one step at a time."* A simple shift in words can make obstacles feel more manageable and within your control.

Why Optimism Matters in Recovery
When navigating recovery, optimism offers a vital lifeline. Addictive behaviors often thrive on feelings of hopelessness and self-doubt. Optimism counters these emotions by reminding you that change is possible and that every step forward matters.

- **It Builds Resilience:** Optimism helps you view setbacks as temporary and manageable, making it easier to stay committed to your goals.

- **It Motivates Action:** When you believe in a better future, you're more likely to take the steps needed to create it.

- **It Strengthens Emotional Health:** By focusing on hope and progress, optimism reduces stress and reinforces a sense of control over your journey.

Optimism doesn't ask you to ignore life's challenges—it empowers you to face them head-on with hope and determination.

By adopting this mindset, you build the resilience to overcome obstacles and the confidence to move toward a brighter future. After all, every challenge is just a chapter, not the whole story—and optimism reminds you that the best pages are still ahead.

Gratitude, Optimism, and the Power of Hope: Keys to Recovery

Hope is not wishful thinking—it's an active force that fuels resilience and drives us forward, even when the path feels uncertain. For those working through recovery or striving to overcome addictive behaviors, cultivating hope becomes a lifeline. It provides the clarity and motivation to stay on the journey, even when setbacks arise. Gratitude and optimism are powerful allies in this process, building the foundation for what Dr. Dan Tomasulo calls *learned hopefulness*—the ability to intentionally nurture hope through mindset and action.

What Is Learned Hopefulness?

Dr. Tomasulo's concept of learned hopefulness teaches us that hope isn't just an emotion; it's a skill you can practice and grow. Through intentional acts of gratitude and optimism, you can train your brain to recognize opportunities and solutions, even during difficult times.

Learned hopefulness invites you to look beyond the immediate struggle, empowering you to believe in the possibility of change and progress. This practice doesn't erase challenges but provides the emotional strength to navigate them with greater clarity and determination.

CHAPTER 6: OPTIMISM AND GRATITUDE

The Connection Between Gratitude, Optimism, and Hope
Gratitude and optimism are essential to cultivating hope, as they work together to shift your focus from what's wrong to what's possible.

- **Gratitude Grounds You in the Present:**
  Gratitude encourages you to acknowledge the good in your life, even in small, simple ways. Whether it's the kindness of a friend or the comfort of a favorite song, this practice helps you recognize moments of joy and stability amidst the chaos. It's the anchor that reminds you, *"Even now, there are things worth appreciating."*

- **Optimism Looks Toward the Future:**
  Optimism, on the other hand, propels you forward. It allows you to reframe setbacks as temporary and challenges as opportunities for growth. For instance, optimism might help you say, *"This is tough, but it's not permanent. I can take steps to move through this."*

Together, gratitude and optimism create a cycle that fuels hope: gratitude helps you see the resources and support you have now, while optimism inspires you to imagine the brighter future you're working toward.

How Gratitude, Optimism, and Hope Support Recovery
Addictive behaviors often stem from feelings of hopelessness, emptiness, or disconnection. Gratitude and optimism counteract these emotions by shifting focus and fostering resilience.

- **Rewiring the Brain for Positivity:**
  Gratitude and optimism activate neural pathways tied to motivation and reward. With regular practice, your brain learns to naturally lean toward positive patterns, reducing the hold of negative thinking.

- **Countering the Negativity Bias:**
  Our brains are wired to focus on potential threats, often amplifying setbacks or challenges. Gratitude and optimism help balance this bias, allowing you to focus on progress and opportunities instead of failures.

- **Providing Emotional Resilience:**
  Recovery is rarely linear, and moments of doubt or temptation are inevitable. Gratitude and optimism offer the strength to view setbacks as part of the process rather than signs of failure.

- **Shifting Focus from Problems to Solutions:**
  Optimism encourages proactive thinking. Instead of dwelling on what went wrong, it prompts you to ask, *"What's the next step I can take?"*

▶ Try This: Cultivate Gratitude, Optimism and Hope Exercise

- **Gratitude Journaling:**
  Each day, write down three things you're grateful for. Focus on specific details—a kind word, a supportive text, or a moment of calm.

- **Reframing Challenges:**
  When facing a setback, ask yourself: *"What can I learn from this?"* Optimism isn't about ignoring hardships; it's about finding meaning in them.

- **Visualizing Success:**
  Spend time imagining a future where you've achieved your recovery goals. How does it feel? What steps did you take to get there? Visualization strengthens hope and motivates action.

- **Acts of Kindness:**
  Helping others nurtures connection and gratitude. Simple gestures, like holding the door for someone or offering a compliment, create ripples of positivity.

- **Daily Affirmations:**
  Remind yourself of your strengths and potential with affirmations like, *"I am capable of growth,"* or *"Each small step brings me closer to my goals."*

Why Optimism and Gratitude Matter in Recovery

Gratitude and optimism don't erase challenges, but they shift the focus. Addiction thrives on hopelessness and disconnection, but these practices remind you of your progress, resources, and capacity for change.

- **Gratitude grounds you in the present,** offering stability during uncertain times.

- **Optimism keeps you looking forward,** inspiring action and perseverance.

- Together, they foster hope—the bridge that connects where you are to where you want to be.

Choosing Hope
Hope is the belief that change is possible, even when the journey feels difficult. By practicing gratitude and optimism, you nurture this belief, transforming challenges into opportunities for growth. Recovery isn't about perfection; it's about progress—and every act of hope brings you closer to the life you envision.

Take a moment today to reflect: *What is one small step I can take to move forward?* By embracing gratitude and optimism, you empower yourself to rise above setbacks and create a future filled with purpose, resilience, and joy.

The Depth of Gratitude: Finding Light in Life's Hardest Moments

Gratitude is often celebrated as a cornerstone of well-being, with research linking it to improved mental health, stronger relationships, and even better physical health. Yet, when life feels overwhelmingly challenging, gratitude can seem out of reach—or even offensive. How can you be thankful when navigating the depths of addictive behaviors?

This is where a deeper, more nuanced form of gratitude steps in: **Level Two Gratitude**, a term coined by John Jeff Hutter in his book *Gutsy Grief*.

Moving Beyond Surface-Level Gratitude
Gratitude at a surface level often focuses on the easy-to-recognize positives, like a sunny day or a delicious meal. While this practice has value, it can feel inadequate or dismissive in moments of profound difficulty. Level Two Gratitude invites you to dig deeper, to find meaning and growth within your challenges—not by sugarcoating them, but by courageously facing them.

Level Two Gratitude allows you to say, *"This is hard, but I am learning."* It acknowledges the rawness of your experience while helping you identify the strength and clarity that often emerge from struggle.

For example, navigating the chaos of addictive behaviors might not feel like something to be grateful for, but you might recognize:

- The resilience you're building.
- The boundaries you're learning to set.
- The deeper understanding you're gaining about yourself.

This form of gratitude doesn't deny the storm; it simply seeks out the small moments of shelter and strength within it.

Why Level Two Gratitude Matters
Gratitude at this deeper level serves as a powerful tool for resilience and healing. It transforms your perspective by focusing on growth rather than loss. When applied to recovery from addictive behaviors, Level Two Gratitude shifts the narrative from self-judgment and shame to self-compassion and progress.

The Science Behind Gratitude
Gratitude is not just a feel-good practice—it has profound psychological and neurological benefits. Studies show that gratitude activates brain regions associated with reward and emotional regulation, reinforcing positivity even during hardship. Level Two Gratitude builds on this foundation, helping to reframe difficulties as opportunities for strength and connection.

Cultivating Level Two Gratitude
Finding gratitude in difficult moments requires intentional effort. Here are ways to start:

1. **Reflect on Growth:** Ask yourself, *What have I learned from this experience? How has it shaped my values or strengths?*

2. **Appreciate Small Wins:** Recognize moments of clarity, connection, or peace, even if they feel fleeting.

3. **Anchor in the Present:** Focus on what is good right now, no matter how small—a kind word, the warmth of a blanket, or a supportive friend.

Try This: Level Two Gratitude Exercise

- **Pause and Reflect:** Think about a challenging situation you're facing.

- **Ask Questions:**
  - What strength have I gained through this?
  - What is one small thing I can appreciate in this moment?
  - How can this experience contribute to my growth?

- **Share Your Gratitude:** If comfortable, share your insights with a trusted friend or loved one.

Reframing Gratitude
Practicing Level Two Gratitude doesn't mean ignoring pain or pretending everything is fine. It's about holding space for both struggle and growth, recognizing that life's hardest moments often teach us the most profound lessons.

In your recovery journey, this perspective can provide hope and motivation. Instead of focusing on what's lost, it shifts attention to what's being gained—strength, clarity, and a deeper connection to yourself.

Level Two Gratitude is not an easy practice, but it's an empowering one. It allows you to acknowledge life's challenges without being consumed by them, offering a pathway to resilience, healing, and growth.

As you move forward, remember: gratitude isn't about ignoring the storm—it's about finding the light that guides you through it. Even in the darkest moments, there are lessons, strengths, and small sparks of joy waiting to be uncovered.

Struggling Well and Post-Traumatic Growth: Turning Pain Into Power

Life's challenges can feel overwhelming, often leaving behind pain and uncertainty. Yet, within these struggles lies the potential for profound growth and transformation. Psychologists Richard Tedeschi and Lawrence Calhoun call this phenomenon *Post-Traumatic Growth* (PTG)—the process of emerging from adversity not just with resilience but with a renewed sense of purpose, strength, and gratitude. Similarly, the concept of *struggling well* offers a framework for embracing hardships as opportunities for self-discovery and growth.

Both PTG and struggling well provide powerful tools for those navigating recovery from addictive behaviors. They teach us that struggles, while painful, can also serve as catalysts for healing, meaning, and lasting change.

The Essence of Post-Traumatic Growth
PTG is more than bouncing back; it's about bouncing forward. It involves positive transformation in key areas of life, including:

- **Appreciation for Life:** Struggles often highlight what truly matters, fostering gratitude for small moments of joy.

- **Strengthened Relationships:** Shared challenges deepen empathy and connection with others.

- **Inner Strength:** Overcoming hardship reveals reserves of resilience and courage.

- **Renewed Purpose:** Adversity often inspires alignment with values and life goals.

- **Spiritual Growth:** Many find a deeper connection to meaning or something greater than themselves.

For individuals in recovery, PTG reframes the journey as one of self-discovery, offering hope that life after hardship can be more meaningful and fulfilling.

Struggling Well: Facing Challenges With Courage
Struggling well doesn't mean avoiding pain—it means transforming it into strength. Like building muscle through stress, struggling well teaches us to grow through life's difficulties. This approach shifts focus from victimhood to empowerment, emphasizing resilience and self-compassion as tools for healing.

When it comes to recovery, struggling well helps:

- **Reframe Setbacks:** Mistakes become opportunities to learn and adapt.

- **Build Resilience:** Each moment of perseverance strengthens your ability to face future challenges.

- **Foster Self-Compassion:** Treating yourself with kindness encourages motivation and commitment.

Why PTG and Struggling Well Matter in Recovery

Addictive behaviors often arise as attempts to numb pain or escape discomfort. PTG and struggling well offer healthier alternatives by encouraging direct engagement with emotions and challenges:

- **Healing Through Pain:** Confronting struggles fosters emotional processing and growth.

- **Building Inner Strength:** Each obstacle overcome reinforces belief in your capacity to grow.

- **Finding Meaning:** Adversity prompts reflection, helping align life with values and priorities.

- **Renewing Hope:** Seeing how struggle leads to growth reinforces the belief in brighter days ahead.

▶ **Try This: Post Traumatic Growth and Struggling Well Exercise**

Both PTG and struggling well can be nurtured through intentional practices:

1. **Reframe Challenges:** Ask yourself, *"What can I learn from this?"* or *"How can this make me stronger?"*

2. **Practice Gratitude:** Focus on lessons, moments of joy, and connections that emerge from hardship.

3. **Seek Meaning:** Reflect on how struggles have shifted your priorities or clarified your goals.

4. **Embrace Self-Compassion:** Treat yourself with kindness and understanding during setbacks.

5. **Build Supportive Connections:** Share your journey with trusted friends or recovery groups to foster mutual growth.

Gratitude, Hope, and Optimism in PTG
PTG is deeply connected to gratitude, hope, and optimism:

- **Gratitude Grounds You:** It helps you recognize the silver linings and moments of growth amidst pain.

- **Hope Fuels Recovery:** Belief in the possibility of a better future inspires perseverance.

- **Optimism Reframes Struggles:** It shifts focus from obstacles to opportunities for growth.

These practices don't deny hardship but integrate it, turning pain into a foundation for strength and resilience.

Embracing Struggle as Growth
Struggling well and PTG remind us that challenges, while difficult, are also transformative. Each setback is an opportunity to

build resilience, deepen self-awareness, and align more closely with your values.

Recovery isn't just about breaking free from harmful patterns—it's about creating a life filled with purpose and strength. Trust in your ability to grow, and know that each step forward brings you closer to the fulfilling life you deserve.

Reflection Question:
What is one challenge that taught you something valuable? By finding meaning in your struggles, you're not just surviving—you're thriving, one moment at a time.

Final Summary

Optimism and gratitude are essential tools for recovery and personal growth. They help us counteract the negativity bias, manage automatic negative thoughts, and challenge cognitive distortions that often fuel addictive behaviors. Optimism keeps us focused on possibilities, fostering hope and motivation, while gratitude anchors us in the present, offering moments of clarity and connection. Together, they rewire our brains for resilience, transform setbacks into stepping stones, and nurture a sense of purpose that supports lasting change.

Cultivating these practices isn't about denying life's difficulties but about finding strength within them. Gratitude teaches us to appreciate what we have, even amidst struggles, and optimism reminds us to believe in a brighter future. When combined, they create a powerful cycle of hope, resilience, and growth, empowering us to thrive—not just survive—on our recovery journey.

Key Takeaways

Optimism and Gratitude Are Grounded in Reality: Optimism and gratitude aren't about ignoring challenges or pretending everything is perfect. Instead, they encourage emotional honesty by acknowledging pain while focusing on growth and meaning. Optimism helps you envision solutions and a brighter future, while gratitude anchors you in the present, finding value in life's moments—even during struggles.

Counteracting Negative Thinking: The negativity bias and automatic negative thoughts (ANTs) can pull focus toward what's wrong, but optimism and gratitude offer a powerful antidote. By reframing challenges and practicing gratitude, you can quiet cognitive distortions like catastrophizing, all-or-nothing thinking, and personalization, creating space for healthier, more constructive self-talk.

Rewiring the Brain for Positivity: Gratitude and optimism have tangible effects on the brain, activating reward pathways and reducing stress. Gratitude reinforces positive behaviors by focusing on what's good in your life, while optimism helps you maintain hope and motivation by shifting your mindset toward proactive solutions.

Supporting Recovery and Well-Being: For those in recovery, optimism and gratitude provide emotional stability and purpose. Gratitude encourages you to sit with your emotions and process them constructively, reducing the pull toward addictive behaviors. Optimism reframes setbacks as opportunities for growth, strengthening your resolve to move forward.

Practical Steps to Cultivate These Practices: Daily practices like journaling three things you're grateful for, reframing challenges with curiosity, and using affirmations or visualizations can transform your mindset. Acts of kindness and mindful reflection deepen these practices, fostering connection and reinforcing your ability to navigate life with resilience and hope.

Hope as the Bridge Between Present and Future: Gratitude grounds you in the present, helping you appreciate your current strengths and resources, while optimism inspires you to envision a better future. Together, they build hope—a dynamic force that fuels recovery and transforms setbacks into stepping stones for growth.

 Optimism and Gratitude Pulse Check

Reflecting on your journey with the RECOVERY Sunshine Assessment, take a moment to evaluate your current level of optimism and gratitude and how they are shaping your well-being and recovery. Consider this a focused check-in on this essential ray of sunshine, offering insight into where you are and where you can cultivate growth.

Ascribe
On a scale of 1–10, how present are optimism and gratitude in your daily life? Use these questions to guide your rating:
- How often do you find yourself focusing on what's possible rather than what's wrong?
- Do you regularly acknowledge the things you're grateful for, even amidst challenges?
- When faced with setbacks, do you believe they are temporary and surmountable?
- How often do you reframe difficult situations with a sense of hope or possibility?
- Do you notice and appreciate small joys or moments of connection throughout your day?

Describe
Reflect on why you gave yourself that score:
- What recent experiences have influenced your ability to practice gratitude and optimism?
- Have you noticed patterns of negative thinking, or have you been able to reframe challenges constructively?

- What moments stand out where you felt particularly hopeful or grateful?
- In what ways have gratitude or optimism helped you navigate a tough situation?

Prescribe

Identify one action you can take to enhance your practice of optimism and gratitude:
- What's one small thing you can do today to express gratitude for someone or something in your life?
- How can you reframe a current challenge to focus on opportunities rather than obstacles?
- What's one positive outcome you can visualize for yourself this week?

Actionable Inspirations

Here are practical ways to strengthen your optimism and gratitude practices:
- Write down three things you're grateful for each day, focusing on small, specific moments.
- Reframe a negative thought by asking, "What's one thing I can learn or gain from this situation?"
- Create a gratitude ritual, like pausing before meals to reflect on something you appreciate.
- Start your day by visualizing one positive outcome or goal you want to work toward.
- Share your gratitude with others through a note, text, or meaningful conversation.

Sentence Completions
Deepen your optimism and gratitude practice with these prompts:

- *A moment I felt truly hopeful was...*
- *Today, I am grateful for...*
- *To cultivate optimism, I will...*
- *A small joy I noticed recently was...*
- *I can reframe this challenge by...*

Mantra for Optimism and Gratitude

"I embrace hope and gratitude, finding strength and joy in each moment."

Or create your own:
_____
_____
_____

A SPARK of HOPE

Your journey is not about perfection; it's about progress, about taking one step at a time toward the life you envision. Optimism doesn't mean you'll never face hardship, and gratitude doesn't mean every day will feel easy. Instead, they remind you that even in the midst of difficulty, there is strength, beauty, and possibility. Trust in your capacity to grow, learn, and overcome. Every small act of gratitude, every moment of hope, is a step forward. You're not just surviving; you're building a life filled with purpose, connection, and joy—and that is something to celebrate. Keep going; you're stronger than you know.

CHAPTER 6: OPTIMISM AND GRATITUDE

What sparked your curiosity or caught your attention?
(Reflect on what you found interesting or intriguing.)

_____
_____
_____
_____
_____

What insights or ideas feel actionable or relevant to your life?
(Identify what you can apply or implement.)

_____
_____
_____
_____
_____

What resonated deeply or felt personally meaningful to you?
(Consider what moved or inspired you emotionally or intellectually.)

_____
_____
_____
_____
_____

CHAPTER 7
Vitality and Health

Your body holds the power to help you heal. *Health and vitality are at the heart of a life well-lived. In recovery, they become even more essential, providing the energy, clarity, and strength to face each day with purpose. Vitality isn't about extreme measures or unattainable ideals; it's about creating a foundation that sustains you—one that honors your body, supports your mind, and uplifts your spirit. Whether it's nourishing yourself with wholesome food, prioritizing restorative sleep, finding joy in movement, or embracing the healing power of touch, each small step toward vitality brings you closer to balance and resilience. In this chapter, we'll explore how these practices can become anchors in your recovery, giving you the strength to build a vibrant and fulfilling life.*

VITALITY AND HEALTH

"Resilience Is About How You Recharge, Not How You Endure." - Shawn Achor

Recovery is a holistic journey that integrates the physical, mental, and emotional aspects of well-being. At its core lies health and vitality—the foundation that empowers you to navigate challenges, build resilience, and thrive. Vitality isn't about striving for perfection or adhering to rigid routines; it's about fostering balance, replenishing your energy, and nurturing your body in ways that sustain you over time.

When you care for your physical health, you enhance your capacity to manage stress, regulate emotions, and stay aligned with your recovery goals. Simple yet transformative practices like nourishing your body with proper nutrition, prioritizing restorative sleep, engaging in regular movement, and embracing meaningful touch are essential tools for creating energy and clarity. These habits don't just heal the body—they also help soothe the nervous system, process stress, and diminish the overwhelm that can fuel addictive behaviors.

In this chapter, we'll explore the science behind vitality, the delicate balance between stress and recovery, and the profound impact of physical health practices on your journey. With research-backed insights and practical strategies, you'll discover how nurturing your body can fuel your recovery and pave the way for a vibrant, balanced, and deeply fulfilling life.

The Secret to Health and Vitality: N.E.S.T (Nutrition, Exercise, Sleep, and Touch)

Recovery from addictive behaviors requires more than just willpower; it demands a holistic approach that nurtures the mind, body, and soul. The N.E.S.T. framework—**Nutrition, Exercise, Sleep, and Touch**—is a foundational concept that supports health and vitality, offering powerful tools to rebuild your life with balance and resilience. Each component plays a crucial role in creating the physical and emotional stability necessary for recovery, reducing the pull toward addictive behaviors, and enhancing overall well-being.

N: Nutrition—Fueling Your Recovery

Nutrition is the cornerstone of physical and mental health. A balanced diet rich in whole foods provides the essential nutrients your body needs to heal and thrive. Research shows that deficiencies in vitamins and minerals, particularly omega-3 fatty acids, B vitamins, and magnesium, can exacerbate anxiety, depression, and temptations—common hurdles in recovery (Sarris et al., 2015).

- **Why It Matters for Recovery**: Proper nutrition stabilizes blood sugar levels, reducing mood swings and irritability. It also supports the production of neurotransmitters like serotonin and dopamine, which regulate mood and reinforce positive behaviors.

- **How to Practice**: Focus on a diet rich in vegetables, fruits, lean proteins, whole grains, and healthy fats. Minimize processed foods and sugars that can contribute to emotional highs and lows.

E: Exercise—A Natural Mood Booster
Regular physical activity is a proven way to improve mood, reduce stress, and enhance cognitive function. Exercise stimulates the release of endorphins, the body's natural "feel-good" chemicals, and increases levels of brain-derived neurotrophic factor (BDNF), which supports brain health and neuroplasticity (Ratey, 2008).

- **Why It Matters for Recovery**: Exercise reduces temptations, alleviates symptoms of withdrawal, and builds resilience by teaching you how to face discomfort and push through challenges. It also offers a healthy outlet for managing stress.

- **How to Practice**: Find an activity you enjoy, whether it's walking, yoga, swimming, or strength training. Aim for at least 30 minutes of moderate exercise most days of the week.

S: Sleep—The Ultimate Recovery Tool
Sleep is the body's natural repair system, essential for both physical and mental recovery. Chronic sleep deprivation is linked to poor decision-making, heightened emotional reactivity, and increased vulnerability to temptations and relapse (Walker, 2017).

- **Why It Matters for Recovery**: Quality sleep enhances emotional regulation, strengthens the immune system, and improves cognitive function, all of which are crucial for navigating the challenges of recovery.

- **How to Practice**: Create a calming bedtime routine, limit screen time before bed, and aim for 7–9 hours of sleep per night. Consider mindfulness or relaxation techniques to ease into restful sleep.

T: Touch—The Healing Power of Connection

Human touch is a basic need that fosters connection, reduces stress, and promotes emotional healing. Physical contact, such as a hug, massage, or even petting an animal, triggers the release of oxytocin, often called the "bonding hormone," which lowers cortisol levels and fosters feelings of trust and safety (Carter, 2014).

- **Why It Matters for Recovery**: Touch provides emotional grounding and reduces the loneliness often associated with addictive behaviors. It strengthens your sense of connection to others and helps regulate emotional states.

- **How to Practice**: Seek out safe, positive forms of physical connection. This could include hugs from loved ones, therapeutic massage, or simply spending time with a pet.

N.E.S.T.: A Framework for Resilience and Recovery

Each element of N.E.S.T. supports the others, creating a synergistic effect that bolsters health and vitality. When you eat well, exercise, sleep soundly, and experience nurturing touch, your body and mind become more resilient to stress and better equipped to overcome the challenges of recovery.

How It Helps With Addictive Behaviors: The N.E.S.T. framework addresses common drivers of addiction—stress, emotional dysregulation, and feelings of disconnection—by providing healthy, sustainable alternatives. It helps restore balance to your life, reinforcing the physical and emotional stability needed to move away from harmful patterns.

Recovery is a journey that involves every aspect of your being. By embracing the N.E.S.T. framework, you give yourself the tools to rebuild your foundation of health and vitality. Nutrition fuels your body, exercise strengthens it, sleep restores it, and touch nurtures your soul. Together, these practices empower you to reclaim your well-being and create a life filled with resilience, connection, and purpose.

Remember, small steps make a big difference. Start where you are, take one step at a time, and trust in the power of N.E.S.T. to guide you toward a brighter, healthier future.

Exercise: The Miracle Drug for Mental Health and Recovery

Exercise is often referred to as a "miracle drug," and for good reason. Dr. John J. Ratey, in his groundbreaking book *Spark: The Revolutionary New Science of Exercise and the Brain*, highlights the profound impact physical activity has on mental health, cognitive function, and emotional resilience. For those navigating recovery from addictive behaviors or managing mental health challenges like depression and anxiety, exercise offers a powerful, accessible tool for transformation.

The Science of Exercise and Mental Health

Dr. Ratey emphasizes that exercise is far more than a tool for physical fitness—it is a catalyst for brain health. Physical activity stimulates the release of endorphins, dopamine, serotonin, and norepinephrine, which are often referred to as "feel-good" chemicals. These neurotransmitters regulate mood, reduce stress, and foster a sense of well-being. In addition, exercise promotes neuroplasticity, the brain's ability to form new neural connections, which is essential for recovery and resilience.

Research supports the idea that regular exercise can:

- **Reduce Depression and Anxiety**: A study published in *JAMA Psychiatry* (2018) found that people who engage in regular physical activity have significantly lower risks of developing depression and anxiety.

- **Improve Cognitive Function**: Exercise boosts brain-derived neurotrophic factor (BDNF), a protein that supports learning, memory, and emotional regulation.

- **Enhance Stress Management**: By lowering cortisol levels, exercise helps the body recover from stress more effectively.

- **Support Recovery from Addictive Behaviors**: Exercise activates the same reward pathways in the brain as addictive substances, providing a healthy, natural alternative for regulating emotions and achieving a sense of reward.

Exercise as a Buffer Against temptations and Relapse
For individuals in recovery from addictive behaviors, exercise plays a dual role. It not only reduces stress and improves mood but also helps counteract the neurochemical imbalances caused by substance use or other addictive behaviors. A 2019 review in *Frontiers in Psychiatry* found that exercise significantly reduces temptations and the risk of relapse by regulating dopamine levels and providing a sense of accomplishment.

Practical Ways to Incorporate Exercise
The beauty of exercise lies in its flexibility—there is no one-size-fits-all approach. Here are ways to integrate movement into your daily life:

Start Small: Even a 10-minute walk can have a positive impact on your mood and energy levels.

Find Joy in Movement: Choose activities you enjoy, whether it's dancing, hiking, yoga, or swimming.

Set Realistic Goals: Focus on consistency rather than intensity. Aim for 150 minutes of moderate activity per week, as recommended by the World Health Organization.

Combine Exercise with Nature: Outdoor activities like jogging or cycling amplify the benefits of movement through exposure to sunlight and green spaces.

Exercise is more than a tool for physical health—it is a vital component of emotional and mental resilience. As Dr. Ratey aptly states, "Exercise is the single best thing you can do for your brain in terms of mood, memory, and learning." For those dealing with depression, anxiety, or recovery from addictive behaviors, exercise offers a transformative path to healing.

Start small, stay consistent, and let movement become your miracle drug. Whether it's a gentle yoga class, a brisk walk, or an intense workout, every step forward brings you closer to a healthier, more balanced life.

The Role of Stress and Recovery: Finding Balance for Vitality and Well-Being

Stress is often cast as the villain in the story of our well-being. But not all stress is bad. In fact, stress, when managed and balanced with recovery, can be a catalyst for growth and resilience. The real challenge lies not in experiencing stress but in the absence of adequate rest and recovery. For those navigating recovery from addictive behaviors, understanding this balance is critical to sustaining health and vitality.

Stress: Friend or Foe?
Stress is a natural response to challenges or demands. It activates the body's "fight or flight" system, releasing hormones like cortisol and adrenaline, which prepare us to face difficulties. This acute stress response is not inherently harmful; it's what has kept humans alive for centuries.

However, when stress becomes chronic and unresolved, it leads to physical, emotional, and psychological strain. Chronic stress contributes to a host of issues, including anxiety, depression, fatigue, and addictive behaviors. Dr. Bessel van der Kolk, in his book *The Body Keeps the Score*, explains how unprocessed stress becomes "trapped" in the body, manifesting as tension, hypervigilance, or even dissociation. Without recovery, the body and mind cannot reset, leading to cycles of imbalance and emotional exhaustion.

The Role of Rest and Recovery
Rest and recovery are the antidote to chronic stress. It is the intentional process of allowing your body and mind to rest, repair, and rejuvenate. Recovery can take many forms, including physical rest, emotional processing, and mental relaxation. It's not about avoiding stress altogether but ensuring that periods of challenge are followed by time for renewal.

For those in recovery from addictive behaviors, incorporating recovery practices is essential to breaking the cycle of stress-induced coping mechanisms. Addictive behaviors often develop as maladaptive responses to unrelieved stress. By prioritizing recovery, you create space to process stress healthily and prevent the need for harmful escapes.

Stress and Recovery in Action: What Science Tells Us
- **The Stress-Resilience Connection**: Studies in psychophysiology show that short-term stress, followed by recovery, strengthens resilience. This concept, known as hormesis, illustrates how manageable doses of stress can make you stronger, much like muscles grow through exercise and rest.

- **Unprocessed Stress and the Body**: Van der Kolk emphasizes that when stress isn't acknowledged and processed, it embeds itself in the body. Practices like mindfulness, yoga, and somatic therapies help release stored tension and reconnect the mind and body.

- **Recovery Reduces Reliance on Maladaptive Coping**: Research in addiction recovery highlights that recovery practices like meditation, sleep hygiene, and restorative activities reduce temptations and the risk of relapse by calming the stress response system.

How to Balance Stress and Recovery
Balancing stress and recovery doesn't require a complete life overhaul. Small, intentional actions can lead to profound effects, creating space for both resilience and restoration. Here's how to get started:

Recognize Your Stress Signals
The first step to managing stress effectively is becoming aware of its presence. Pay attention to physical and emotional signs, such as tightness in your chest, irritability, or persistent fatigue. Awareness helps you identify when it's time to take action and prevent stress from building up unchecked.

Prioritize Restorative Practices
Recovery encompasses physical, mental, and emotional well-being. Addressing all three aspects ensures a comprehensive approach:

- **Physical Recovery**: Ensure you get regular sleep, engage in gentle movement, and consume nourishing meals. These foundational habits support your body's ability to recover from stress.

- **Mental Recovery**: Engage in practices like meditation, journaling, or spending time in nature. These activities calm your nervous system, creating mental clarity and reducing the cognitive load stress can bring.

- **Emotional Recovery**: Take time to process your feelings through therapy, meaningful conversations, or creative outlets. Expressing emotions rather than suppressing them helps resolve underlying tension.

Engage in Mind-Body Practices
Mind-body practices like yoga, deep breathing, and mindfulness are powerful tools for releasing stress stored in the body. These techniques reconnect you to your physical self, enabling you to process and let go of tension. As Dr. Bessel van der Kolk highlights in *The Body Keeps the Score*, such practices play a vital role in emotional and physical recovery.

Build a Recovery Routine
Consistency is key to balancing stress and recovery. Schedule time for restorative activities daily, even if it's just a 10-minute walk or a few minutes of mindful breathing. These small but consistent habits create a protective buffer against stress, ensuring you maintain vitality and well-being.

By incorporating these practices into your life, you'll create a sustainable rhythm that helps you navigate stress while staying grounded in your recovery journey.

Recovery and Addictive Behaviors
Unresolved stress often drives addictive behaviors as individuals seek quick relief from discomfort. By creating a balance between stress and recovery, you can address the underlying causes of stress without turning to harmful coping mechanisms. Recovery allows you to replace short-term escapes with sustainable practices that build emotional resilience and inner strength.

For example:
- **Sleep**: A consistent sleep schedule reduces cortisol levels and improves emotional regulation, making it easier to resist temptations.

- **Physical Activity**: Exercise releases endorphins and reduces tension, providing a healthy outlet for stress.

- **Mindfulness**: Practicing mindfulness builds awareness of triggers and stressors, enabling thoughtful responses instead of reactive behaviors.

The Key to Vitality
Stress is an inevitable part of life, but it doesn't have to derail your well-being. The secret lies in honoring the balance between challenge and recovery. By allowing yourself to rest, process, and restore, you build the emotional and physical resilience needed to thrive.

As van der Kolk reminds us, "The body keeps the score." When stress is acknowledged and recovery prioritized, the score becomes one of growth, vitality, and lasting transformation. For those on the recovery journey, this balance is not just beneficial—it's essential. With intentional recovery practices, you create a life where stress fuels resilience, not relapse, and where challenges become stepping stones toward a healthier, more vibrant future.

The Power of Self-Regulation: Overcoming Ego Depletion and Boosting Vitality in Recovery

Self-regulation is the foundation of emotional well-being and a critical skill for managing addictive behaviors. It empowers you to resist immediate impulses, manage emotions, and make choices aligned with your long-term goals. But self-regulation isn't infinite—a concept known as **ego depletion** reminds us that our mental resources can be temporarily drained. This interplay between self-regulation, ego depletion, and vitality reveals pathways to creating a balanced and resilient life in recovery.

What Is Self-Regulation, and Why Is It Important?
Self-regulation is your ability to consciously guide thoughts, emotions, and actions, particularly in the face of stress or temptation. For anyone navigating recovery, this skill is essential for breaking old patterns and building healthier habits.

Think of **Walter Mischel's marshmallow test**, where children who delayed gratification by waiting for a second marshmallow often went on to achieve greater success in life. That same ability to pause, reflect, and make intentional choices is what self-regulation brings to recovery. For example, when a craving or emotional trigger arises, self-regulation helps you pause, take a deep breath, and choose a coping mechanism that supports your recovery rather than undermining it.

The Challenge of Ego Depletion
Ego depletion occurs when the mental effort required for self-control becomes temporarily exhausted. Picture this: You've spent all day managing emotions, making decisions, or resisting temptations. By the evening, your mental reserves are depleted, leaving you more vulnerable to impulsive choices.

Psychologist Roy Baumeister's research reveals that self-regulation functions like a muscle—it gets tired when overused but can also be strengthened over time. In recovery, this means that a particularly tough day might leave you less capable of resisting temptations. Recognizing ego depletion is key to understanding why some moments feel harder than others and why replenishing your energy is crucial.

Vitality: Replenishing Your Mental and Physical Energy
Vitality is the antidote to ego depletion. As Kelly McGonigal explains in *The Willpower Instinct*, replenishing your mental and physical resources is essential to maintaining self-regulation. When you prioritize practices that boost energy and well-being, you enhance your capacity to navigate challenges with clarity and resilience.

Key strategies to enhance vitality include:

Sleep: Sleep is the ultimate recovery tool, restoring cognitive and emotional energy. As Matthew Walker highlights in *Why We Sleep*, even a single night of poor sleep can impair self-regulation and decision-making.

- **Nutrition**: A balanced diet stabilizes blood sugar, supporting steady energy and emotional regulation. Deficiencies in key nutrients like omega-3s and magnesium can exacerbate mood swings and temptations.

- **Exercise**: Physical activity boosts neurotransmitters like dopamine and serotonin, which improve mood, reduce stress, and enhance self-regulation. As John Ratey describes in *Spark*, exercise primes the brain for better decision-making.

- **Mindfulness**: Practices like meditation and deep breathing increase awareness of your thoughts and emotions, allowing you to respond with intention rather than react impulsively.

Why Self-Regulation Matters in Recovery
Self-regulation is the bridge between emotional triggers and thoughtful responses. It creates a pause—a moment to choose actions aligned with your goals instead of succumbing to old habits. This pause is transformative in recovery, where the pull toward addictive behaviors often feels automatic.

By practicing self-regulation consistently, you strengthen the neural pathways that support positive behaviors, making them more natural over time. Additionally, each small victory—resisting a temptation, navigating a stressful situation—reinforces your belief in your ability to change. This cumulative effect empowers you to break free from destructive cycles and build a sustainable, thriving life.

A Vital Life Supports Lasting Recovery
Recovery is not just about managing impulses; it's about cultivating vitality, resilience, and purpose. By understanding how self-regulation works, addressing ego depletion, and investing in your physical and emotional energy, you build a foundation for lasting change.

As Kelly McGonigal reminds us, self-regulation is not about being perfect; it's about learning to navigate each moment with curiosity and self-compassion. Remember, every time you pause, reflect, and choose a path that supports your recovery, you are strengthening your ability to thrive. With practice, self-regulation becomes not just a skill but a superpower that transforms challenges into opportunities for growth and healing.

Vitality and Health: Navigating Trauma, Triggers, and Stress

Vitality is your lifeline—the physical, mental, and emotional energy you need to live fully and recover effectively from life's challenges. When managing recovery or addictive behaviors, cultivating vitality becomes crucial for navigating stress, trauma, and triggers. Building vitality isn't just about feeling energized—it's about creating a foundation for resilience, emotional regulation, and a healthier relationship with yourself.

The Connection Between Stress, Trauma, and Triggers

Stress is a natural response to life's demands, but chronic stress can overwhelm both your body and mind, especially if you're carrying unresolved trauma. Trauma leaves a lasting imprint on the nervous system, often keeping you stuck in a heightened state of fight-or-flight. Triggers—whether external events or internal emotions—can activate this stress response, leaving you feeling overwhelmed and at risk of falling back into harmful coping patterns.

Down-Regulating Your Nervous System

To break the cycle of stress and trauma, learning how to down-regulate your nervous system is essential. Down-regulation helps calm the body's stress response, allowing you to feel balanced and safe again. Activating the parasympathetic nervous system—the body's rest-and-digest mode—creates space for recovery and resilience.

Here's how down-regulation supports your vitality:

1. **Calms Emotional Reactivity:** A regulated nervous system allows you to pause before reacting to triggers, empowering you to make healthier decisions.

2. **Enhances Recovery:** Stress reduction creates the conditions for physical and emotional healing, replenishing the energy drained by trauma and chronic stress.

3. **Builds Resilience:** Consistent down-regulation strengthens your capacity to manage challenges without resorting to harmful habits.

▶ **Try This: Navigating Stress, Trauma and Triggers Exercise**

1. **Mind-Body Practices:** Techniques like yoga, mindfulness meditation, and deep breathing directly calm your nervous system. These practices lower cortisol levels, alleviate anxiety, and release stress stored in the body, as described by Dr. Bessel van der Kolk in *The Body Keeps the Score*.

2. **Grounding Techniques:** When faced with a trigger, grounding exercises—like focusing on your breath or naming five things you can see—help bring you back to the present moment, so you can regain control.

3. **Physical Activity:** Movement is one of the most powerful tools you have to relieve stress. Exercise not only releases endorphins but also helps process the physical tension that trauma creates. Dr. John Ratey, in *Spark*, highlights how exercise transforms brain function, making it an essential part of recovery.

4. **Creative Expression:** Art, music, journaling, or other creative outlets allow you to process emotions and release tension. Creativity can act as a bridge between your internal experiences and external understanding, fostering healing.

5. **Safe Connections:** Positive relationships reduce stress and help regulate your nervous system. When you feel supported and understood, oxytocin—the bonding hormone—is released, promoting calm and trust.

6. **Establish Routines:** Consistency helps your nervous system feel safe. Building daily rituals—like a morning stretch or an evening gratitude practice—provides stability and a sense of control.

Building Vitality Through Recovery
Vitality isn't just about reducing stress—it's about actively recovering. By down-regulating your nervous system, you create the physical and emotional energy to navigate life's challenges without falling into reactive patterns. This process involves embracing balance: allowing yourself to rest, process emotions, and rebuild after stressful moments.

Recovery isn't about avoiding triggers altogether—it's about cultivating the tools to face them with clarity and compassion. Every moment of recovery reinforces the neural pathways for resilience and vitality, making healthier choices feel more natural and achievable over time.

Why Vitality Matters
Investing in your vitality empowers you to live fully, rather than merely surviving. It helps you face the complexities of trauma, triggers, and stress with strength and intention, rather than resorting to harmful habits. When you focus on your vitality, you're not just managing recovery—you're thriving within it.

By prioritizing vitality, you're building a foundation of strength, resilience, and balance that sustains your recovery. Through tools like mindfulness, movement, and connection, you can navigate life's stressors while honoring your well-being. Remember, recovery is a journey of small, intentional steps, and every act of self-care brings you closer to the life of health and vitality you deserve.

Breathwork: A Vital Tool for Health, Vitality, and Recovery

Breathwork is one of the simplest yet most transformative practices available for enhancing health, vitality, and emotional balance. As Dr. Andrew Huberman, neuroscientist and host of *The Huberman Lab Podcast*, explains, intentional breathing techniques directly influence the nervous system, allowing us to regulate stress and emotional states effectively. For those navigating recovery from addictive behaviors, breathwork offers a powerful way to manage stress, reduce temptations, and cultivate mindfulness. Grounded in science, breathwork engages the body and mind in ways that promote resilience, healing, and self-awareness.

The Science Behind Breathwork
Intentional breathing directly impacts the nervous system by activating the parasympathetic "rest-and-digest" response, countering the effects of stress and trauma. Research has shown that breathwork can:

- **Reduce Stress:** Studies confirm that controlled breathing lowers cortisol levels, calming the body and mind (Brown & Gerbarg, 2005).

- **Enhance Emotional Regulation:** Breathing techniques have been linked to improved emotional resilience, helping individuals process and release stored trauma (van der Kolk, 2014).

- **Support Recovery:** Deep breathing has been found to reduce anxiety, which often underpins addictive behaviors, providing a healthier coping mechanism (Schnabel et al., 2018).

▶ Try This: Breathwork Exercise

There are many breathing exercises to try, each offering unique benefits. Experiment with these techniques to discover what resonates with you:

Box Breathing (Four-Square Breathing):
- Inhale for a count of four.
- Hold your breath for four.
- Exhale for four.
- Hold your breath for four again. This technique calms the mind and body, making it ideal for managing stress and temptations.

Diaphragmatic (Belly) Breathing:
- Place one hand on your chest and the other on your belly.

- Inhale deeply through your nose, allowing your belly to rise.
- Exhale slowly through your mouth, letting your belly fall. This practice reconnects you to your body and promotes deep relaxation.

Ujjayi Pranayama (Victorious Breath):
- Inhale deeply through your nose, slightly constricting your throat to create a gentle ocean-like sound.
- Exhale through your nose with the same constriction. This breathing style, commonly used in yoga, calms the nervous system and enhances vitality.

Three Deep Breaths (Thomas Crum):
- Take one deep breath to let go of tension.
- Take another to center yourself in the present moment.
- Take a third to focus on what truly matters to you. This practice is a quick way to reset and refocus during stressful moments.

Breathwork and Recovery
Breathwork is especially valuable for those in recovery because it offers immediate, accessible relief from stress and triggers.

Here's how it helps:
- **Navigating Triggers:** When faced with temptations, breathwork creates a pause, allowing you to respond thoughtfully rather than react impulsively.

- **Processing Stress and Trauma:** Intentional breathing helps release tension stored in the body, fostering emotional healing and balance.

- **Promoting Mindfulness:** By focusing on the breath, you strengthen your ability to stay present, reducing reliance on harmful coping mechanisms.

Finding What Works for You
With so many breathing exercises available, the key is to find the one that works best for you. Each technique offers unique benefits, so explore and see which fits seamlessly into your routine. Consistency matters more than perfection—regular practice amplifies the benefits over time.

Breathwork is a natural, science-backed tool that enhances health, vitality, and recovery. It empowers you to take control of your emotional and physical well-being, offering a reliable anchor during challenging times. Whether it's three deep breaths to ground yourself or a deeper practice like Ujjayi Pranayama, every intentional breath is a step toward resilience, healing, and freedom.

As you navigate your recovery journey, let breathwork remind you of the strength and balance already within you—one breath at a time.

Final Summary

Vitality and health are the foundation of a thriving recovery journey, providing the energy and resilience needed to navigate life's challenges. When you nurture your body through balanced nutrition, restorative sleep, regular exercise, and meaningful touch, you're building a strong foundation for emotional resilience, mental clarity, and long-term well-being. The vitality practices explored in this chapter not only replenish your energy but also empower you to navigate triggers, reduce stress, and cultivate the strength needed to sustain positive change. Each step you take toward supporting your health brings you closer to a life of balance and thriving.

.... **Key Takeaways** ....

The N.E.S.T. Framework Supports Holistic Health: The N.E.S.T. framework—Nutrition, Exercise, Sleep, and Touch—emphasizes the importance of addressing physical, mental, and emotional needs. By nourishing your body with whole foods, staying active, prioritizing rest, and fostering connection through touch, you create a foundation for sustained recovery and vitality.

Self-Regulation is Essential for Resilience: Self-regulation enables you to manage emotions, impulses, and actions, particularly in the face of triggers or stress. Understanding the concept of ego depletion reminds us that self-control is finite but replenishable. Practices like mindfulness, quality sleep, and balanced nutrition help restore the mental resources needed for self-regulation.

Breathwork Enhances Recovery and Resilience: Breathwork is a simple yet powerful tool for regulating the nervous system and managing emotional states. By engaging in intentional breathing techniques, you can reduce stress, improve focus, and strengthen your ability to navigate cravings and temptations during recovery.

Vitality Fuels Long-Term Recovery: Vitality—your overall physical and emotional energy—is critical for sustaining recovery. Practices such as regular exercise, proper sleep, and healthy nutrition enhance your resilience and provide the energy needed to overcome challenges. When vitality is prioritized, recovery becomes a process of thriving, not just surviving.

A Balanced Life Supports Recovery Goals: Recovery isn't solely about avoiding harmful behaviors; it's about creating a life that nurtures your well-being. By focusing on vitality and integrating supportive practices like breathwork and the N.E.S.T. framework, you build a life of balance, purpose, and strength, reducing the pull of addictive behaviors.

 Vitality and Health Pulse Check

Reflecting on your journey with the RECOVERY Sunshine Assessment, take a moment to evaluate your current level of vitality and how it is supporting your well-being and recovery. Consider this a focused check-in on this foundational ray of sunshine, offering insight into how well you are nurturing your physical and emotional health and where you can grow.

Ascribe
On a scale of 1–10, how well are you supporting your vitality through health-focused practices? Use these questions to guide your rating:
- How balanced is your nutrition, and how consistently do you fuel your body with nourishing foods?
- Are you incorporating regular movement or exercise that uplifts your energy and mood?
- Do you consistently get quality, restorative sleep to recharge your body and mind?
- How often do you experience meaningful physical connection, such as touch or closeness with loved ones or pets?
- Are you intentional about reducing stress and creating time for recovery and rejuvenation?

Describe
Reflect on why you gave yourself that score:
- What recent habits or choices have contributed to your sense of vitality?
- Are there areas, such as sleep or nutrition, where you've struggled or could prioritize more?

- How has physical movement or connection impacted your mood and energy levels?
- What moments stand out where you felt particularly energized, grounded, or balanced?

Prescribe

Identify one action you can take to enhance your vitality:
- What's one small change you can make to your daily routine to support your nutrition or exercise?
- How can you create a more consistent sleep schedule or improve your sleep environment?
- What's one way you can invite meaningful touch into your life today, such as a hug or a massage?
- How can you introduce a moment of mindfulness or relaxation into your day to reduce stress?

Actionable Inspirations

Here are practical ways to prioritize vitality and health:
- Plan your meals for the week, focusing on whole, nutrient-dense foods that energize your body.
- Set a consistent bedtime and create a calming pre-sleep routine, such as reading or meditating.
- Commit to a 10-minute walk or stretch session each day to move your body and clear your mind.
- Schedule time for a meaningful connection, whether it's a hug, a chat with a friend, or time with your pet.
- Take a moment each evening to reflect on one way you supported your health that day.

Sentence Completions
Deepen your connection to vitality with these prompts:

- A choice I made today that supported my health was…
- When I feel energized, I notice that I…
- To improve my well-being this week, I will…
- One way I can bring more balance to my life is…
- I feel most vital when I…

Mantra for Vitality and Health
"My body is my foundation, and I honor it with nourishment, movement, and rest."

Or create your own:
_____
_____
_____

A SPARK of HOPE

Your body is your ally in this journey—a powerful resource waiting to be nurtured and supported. Every mindful meal, restful night, or moment of joyful movement is a declaration of care and commitment to yourself. Even the smallest choices, like taking a deep breath or pausing to rest, can ripple outward, creating strength and clarity. Remember, vitality is not a destination but a daily practice—a way to recharge, restore, and align with the life you're building. Trust in your ability to honor your body and its needs, and know that each step forward is a step toward wholeness. You've got this, and your journey to health and vitality is already underway.

What sparked your curiosity or caught your attention?
(Reflect on what you found interesting or intriguing.)
_____
_____
_____
_____
_____

What insights or ideas feel actionable or relevant to your life?
(Identify what you can apply or implement.)
_____
_____
_____
_____
_____

What resonated deeply or felt personally meaningful to you?
(Consider what moved or inspired you emotionally or intellectually.)
_____
_____
_____
_____
_____

CHAPTER 8

Engagement and Purpose

A life filled with purpose is a life well-lived. Engagement and purpose are the heartbeat of a meaningful life. They give us something to wake up for, something to work toward, and a reason to persevere through life's inevitable challenges. When you reconnect with what excites you and align your actions with your values, you create a sense of fulfillment that outshines even the hardest days. In recovery, engagement and purpose aren't just nice-to-haves—they are transformative tools that fill the void left by harmful habits and bring you closer to the life you truly want to live. This chapter will guide you in discovering what lights you up and how to use that spark to create a life of joy, direction, and resilience.

ENGAGEMENT AND PURPOSE

"The purpose of life is not to be happy.
It is to be useful, to be honorable, to be compassionate,
to have it make some difference that you have lived
and lived well." – Ralph Waldo Emerson

Recovery isn't just about leaving addictive behaviors behind—it's about rediscovering the richness of life, embracing meaningful activities, and reconnecting with your sense of purpose. Engagement and purpose are transformative forces that help fill the void left by harmful habits, channeling your energy into pursuits that bring joy, creativity, and direction.

Engagement invites you to fully immerse yourself in activities that spark passion and vitality, while purpose provides the deeper "why" behind these actions. Together, they form a framework for living with resilience and meaning, empowering you to navigate challenges and sustain recovery.

These aren't just tools for overcoming addiction; they're pathways to a more vibrant, fulfilling life. By anchoring you in what truly matters, engagement and purpose offer the strength to rise above harmful patterns and step into a life of intention, connection, and hope. This chapter will guide you in unlocking these transformative forces, helping you create a life that reflects your values and inspires lasting change.

The Power of Purpose: A Pathway to Well-Being and Resilience

Purpose isn't just a guiding principle—it's a driving force that connects us to meaning and fulfillment. As Viktor Frankl famously wrote in *Man's Search for Meaning*, "Life is never made unbearable by circumstances, but only by lack of meaning and purpose." Purpose provides direction, helps us navigate challenges, and aligns our actions with our values.

Why Purpose Matters for Well-Being
Research consistently shows that having a sense of purpose boosts resilience, lowers anxiety and depression, and even extends longevity. Purpose acts as an emotional anchor, providing clarity and grounding during uncertain times. As Angela Duckworth highlights in *Grit*, purpose fuels perseverance toward meaningful goals, transforming challenges into stepping stones.

Purpose as a Buffer Against Addictive Behaviors
Addiction often thrives in the absence of meaning, as individuals turn to unhealthy habits to fill an emotional void. Purpose counters this by offering:

- **Direction:** A focus on long-term goals makes it easier to resist temptations.

- **Resilience:** Purpose motivates you to endure and grow through challenges.

- **Self-Worth:** A meaningful life reminds you that you matter, reducing reliance on harmful behaviors for validation.

Johann Hari's work on addiction reminds us that purpose and connection are antidotes to the aimlessness that often leads to harmful behaviors.

Try This: Discovering Your Purpose Exercise

Finding purpose is a personal journey, but Simon Sinek's advice from *Start With Why* is a great starting point: "People don't buy what you do; they buy why you do it." To uncover your "why," consider:

- **Reflecting on Your Values:** Ask, "What truly matters to me?"

- **Exploring Your Passions:** Engage in activities that bring you joy.

- **Looking Beyond Yourself:** Find ways to positively impact others.

- **Embracing Growth:** Purpose evolves as you do; stay open to new possibilities.

Purpose in Action: Small Steps with Big Impact
Purpose doesn't need to be grand to be transformative. Start with small, meaningful actions:

- Volunteer for a cause you care about.
- Set a personal goal and take consistent steps toward it.
- Create something that brings joy to yourself and others.
- Build relationships that align with your values.

Purpose as a Lifelong Guide
Purpose isn't static—it's a journey. Brene Brown reminds us that living a purposeful life requires vulnerability and courage. Recovery becomes more than overcoming the past—it's about crafting a future filled with meaning and authenticity.

Purpose is your compass, guiding you through setbacks and helping you reframe challenges as part of a greater story. It doesn't have to be grand or perfect; it just needs to resonate with who you are and the life you want to create.

Discovering Ikigai: Unlocking Your Unique Purpose and Meaning

In the pursuit of a meaningful and fulfilling life, many people look to the Japanese concept of **ikigai**, which translates to "reason for being." Ikigai is more than just a philosophical idea; it's a practical framework for understanding what drives you, what gives you joy, and how you can connect with your purpose. By helping you identify the intersection of your passions, skills, contributions to the world, and what you love, ikigai fosters a deep sense of engagement and meaning in life.

What Is Ikigai?
Ikigai is a synthesis of four core elements:

1. **What You Love** *(Passion)*: Activities or interests that bring you joy and make you feel alive.

2. **What You're Good At** *(Profession)*: Your unique talents and abilities.

3. **What the World Needs** *(Mission)*: How you can make a difference or contribute to others.

4. **What You Can Be Paid For** *(Vocation)*: Opportunities to sustain your life financially.

Your ikigai lies at the intersection of these elements, representing the sweet spot where what you love, what you're good at, what the world needs, and what you can be paid for come together in harmony.

How Ikigai Helps You Engage with Life
1. **Promotes Self-Discovery**
   The process of identifying your ikigai requires self-reflection and exploration. This deeper understanding of your values, passions, and strengths allows you to connect with your authentic self.

2. **Fosters Daily Engagement**
   Ikigai isn't about achieving monumental goals; it's about finding joy and meaning in the small, everyday moments. Whether it's through meaningful work, relationships, or hobbies, ikigai encourages you to engage fully with life.

3. **Cultivates Purpose**
   Knowing your ikigai gives you a clear sense of direction and purpose, helping you prioritize activities that align with your values and bring fulfillment.

4. Strengthens Resilience
Having a purpose rooted in your ikigai serves as an anchor during challenging times. It motivates you to overcome obstacles, knowing that your actions are meaningful and aligned with your life's mission.

Ikigai and Recovery
For those navigating recovery or seeking to move away from addictive behaviors, ikigai offers a powerful tool to reframe your life. Addictive behaviors often fill a void or serve as an escape from feelings of disconnection or lack of purpose. Ikigai helps fill that void with meaningful activities and goals that bring joy and fulfillment.

- **Focus on What You Love**: Rediscover passions that may have been overshadowed by addictive behaviors.

- **Tap into Your Strengths**: Recognize your unique talents and how they can contribute to your recovery journey.

- **Contribute to Others**: Helping others or engaging in meaningful work fosters a sense of connection and purpose.

- **Engage with Life Fully**: By aligning your daily actions with your ikigai, you replace harmful habits with intentional and life-affirming practices.

Try This: Find Your Ikigai Exercise

Reflect on Your Passions
Ask yourself: What activities make me lose track of time? What do I love doing purely for the joy it brings?

Identify Your Strengths
Consider: What am I naturally good at? What skills or talents do others recognize in me?

Consider the World's Needs
Reflect on: How can I contribute to my community or make a difference in the lives of others?

Explore Sustainability
Ask: What opportunities align with my passions and skills that can also support my life financially?

Ikigai in Action
Imagine you love teaching (what you love), have a talent for simplifying complex ideas (what you're good at), find joy in empowering others (what the world needs), and work as a coach or mentor (what you can be paid for). These overlapping areas create your ikigai—a life infused with purpose, meaning, and engagement.

Ikigai is not about perfection or a single life-defining purpose; it's about living intentionally and aligning your actions with what truly matters to you. By connecting with your ikigai, you cultivate a sense of fulfillment that helps you engage more deeply with life, build resilience, and create a foundation for well-being. Whether you're navigating recovery or seeking to enhance your sense of purpose, ikigai offers a roadmap to a life that feels vibrant, meaningful, and uniquely yours.

Tapping Into Your Why: Reclaiming Purpose After Disengagement

Discovering your "why"—the core reason that drives your actions and decisions—is a deeply personal journey, especially after a period of disengagement. While purpose provides overarching direction, your "why" offers clarity and motivation in the day-to-day moments that shape your life. Viktor Frankl, renowned psychiatrist and author of *Man's Search for Meaning*, reminds us that having a "why" can help us endure almost any "how." It's this sense of purpose that transforms struggles into stepping stones toward a meaningful life.

When navigating addictive behaviors, reconnecting with your "why" is especially powerful. It shifts focus from simply overcoming addictive behaviors to embracing a life filled with intentionality, engagement, and hope. Your "why" becomes a beacon, illuminating the path forward, even when the journey feels uncertain.

Rebuilding Your Why After Disengagement
If you've felt stuck or disconnected, take heart—rediscovering your "why" is a process, not a destination. Here are practical steps to help you reconnect with your deeper purpose:

1. **Reflect on Past Joys**
   Consider moments when you felt alive and fulfilled. What activities, relationships, or experiences brought you a sense of meaning? These memories can offer valuable insights into your "why."

2. **Reconnect with Core Values**
   Purpose is rooted in what matters most to you. Reflect on your values:

   - What do you stand for?

   - What principles guide your decisions?
     For example, values like kindness, creativity, or perseverance might align with your purpose and help define your "why."

3. **Embrace Contribution**
   As we explored in the Ikigai exercise, purpose often involves service to others or connection to a larger whole. Ask yourself:

   - How can I use my strengths to benefit others?

   - What unique perspectives or skills can I share?
     Small acts of contribution can reignite a sense of meaning and belonging.

4. **Start Small and Stay Curious**
   If your purpose feels elusive, don't wait for a grand revelation. Try volunteering, taking up a hobby, or

joining a supportive community. These small actions can spark clarity and build momentum toward rediscovering your "why."

Why Your Why Matters in Recovery
Reconnecting with your "why" is particularly impactful for those in recovery. It shifts the focus from what you're trying to avoid to what you're striving to build, fostering a mindset of growth and self-discovery.

- **From Avoidance to Intention**: Instead of focusing solely on avoiding harmful behaviors, your "why" encourages meaningful actions that align with your values.

- **From Isolation to Connection**: Purpose often involves connection, fostering relationships that bring support and belonging.

- **From Hopelessness to Hope**: A clear "why" transforms setbacks into opportunities for growth, reminding you that your journey holds meaning.

Your "why" is uniquely yours, shaped by your experiences, values, and aspirations. It doesn't need to be grand or world-changing—it simply needs to resonate with who you are and the life you want to create. Whether it's supporting others, pursuing a passion, or embracing the beauty of each day, your "why" will guide you forward.

Take small steps, stay curious, and trust that as you engage with life, your purpose will become clearer. In reconnecting with your "why," you'll not only rediscover meaning but also build a life that aligns with your values, strengths, and dreams.

Tapping Into Flow and Joy: The Power of Purposeful Engagement

Engagement is about immersing yourself in activities that ignite passion, focus, and joy. Psychologist Mihaly Csikszentmihalyi, who coined the term "flow," describes it as a state of optimal engagement where challenge and skill are perfectly balanced. In recovery, tapping into flow can provide a sense of purpose and fulfillment, replacing destructive patterns with life-affirming experiences.

The Science of Flow and Recovery

Flow isn't just about enjoying an activity—it has profound psychological and physiological benefits that support recovery:

- **Boosts Dopamine Naturally:** Flow states elevate dopamine levels, a neurotransmitter that addictive behaviors often exploit. This creates a healthy, sustainable way to experience pleasure.

- **Reduces Stress:** Engaging in meaningful activities calms the nervous system, helping you manage triggers and emotional challenges more effectively.

- **Builds Self-Esteem:** Accomplishing tasks that align with your skills and values reinforces confidence and personal growth.

Try This: Cultivating Flow Exercise

1. **Identify What Sparks Joy**
   Think about activities that naturally draw you in and make time disappear. It could be painting, writing, gardening, hiking, or even solving complex problems. Rediscovering hobbies or exploring new ones can uncover sources of flow.

2. **Balance Challenge and Skill**
   Flow occurs when a task is challenging enough to stretch your abilities but not so difficult that it feels overwhelming. Seek out activities that push your limits just enough to keep you engaged.

3. **Prioritize Purposeful Activities**
   Choose activities that align with your values and goals. Doing what matters to you fosters a deeper connection to your life's purpose and keeps you motivated to move forward.

Why Flow Matters in Recovery

Flow provides a powerful alternative to the highs and lows of addictive behaviors. By engaging in activities that align with your purpose and joy, you create positive experiences that regulate emotions, enhance well-being, and foster long-term resilience.

Flow transforms recovery from a struggle into an opportunity for growth, joy, and personal fulfillment. Embrace activities that captivate your attention and bring you peace—you'll find they become essential tools for living a vibrant and meaningful life.

The Power of Play: Bringing Purpose, Joy, and Fun into Your Life

Play is often dismissed as something reserved for children, but research tells a different story. Play is a fundamental human need, essential for well-being, connection, and even purpose. In *The Power of Play*, a book by Dr. Elaine O'Brien and myself, we explore how engaging in playful activities can enrich your life, ignite joy, and deepen your sense of purpose. Play is a powerful pathway to vitality, creativity, and connection, making it an essential tool for living a vibrant and meaningful life.

Why Play Matters
Play is not a frivolous activity—it is a meaningful way to connect with yourself and others, enhance your mental health, and bring joy into your daily life. Here's why play is so powerful:

- **It Boosts Emotional Well-Being:** Play releases endorphins, reduces stress, and fosters resilience. It creates a space where you can experience unfiltered joy and emotional release.

- **It Enhances Social Connection:** Whether it's a game night with friends or a shared creative project, play builds bonds and fosters trust and collaboration.

- **It Ignites Creativity and Problem-Solving:** Engaging in playful activities encourages you to think outside the box, approach challenges with curiosity, and discover new ways to engage with life.

- **It Provides a Sense of Purpose:** Play connects you to your passions, helping you rediscover what lights you up and gives meaning to your days.

▶ **Try This: Foster Play, Purpose and Joy Exercise**

Incorporating play into your life isn't just about having fun—it's about reconnecting with your inner spark. For those navigating recovery or seeking to prevent addictive behaviors, play can be a lifeline:

1. **Rekindle What Brings You Joy**
   Reflect on the activities you loved as a child or hobbies you've always wanted to try. Whether it's painting, dancing, or building something with your hands, these moments of play can reignite passion and excitement.

2. **Build Connection Through Play**
   Play with others fosters community and shared experiences. Activities like team sports, board games, or collaborative art projects create opportunities for meaningful connection and joy.

3. **Embrace Playful Movement**
   Dr. Elaine O'Brien highlights the link between play and

physical vitality. Activities like dancing, hiking, or even playful yoga flows bring movement and joy together, enhancing both physical and emotional well-being.

4. **Explore New Forms of Play**
   Sometimes we lose touch with play because it feels unfamiliar as adults. Try experimenting with improvisation, exploring nature, or engaging in playful problem-solving to discover new ways to bring joy into your life.

Play in Recovery: A Tool for Growth

Play is a powerful counter to the rigidity and stress that often accompany recovery. It shifts your focus from what you're moving away from (addictive behaviors) to what you're moving toward—a life filled with purpose, joy, and connection. Play fosters self-expression and helps you experience the moment without judgment, making it a valuable tool for emotional resilience and growth.

Rediscovering the Joy of Play

To make play a part of your life, start small. Incorporate playful moments into your daily routine—play catch, doodle on a piece of paper, or simply laugh at something funny. These small acts of play can have a profound impact on your overall sense of well-being and engagement with life.

As *The Power of Play* explains, "Play connects us to our best selves, our loved ones, and to life itself." Embracing play is not just about having fun—it's about reclaiming joy, building resilience, and living with purpose.

So, take a moment to laugh, create, explore, or connect. Let play remind you that life isn't just about surviving—it's about thriving, with purpose and joy lighting the way.

Living Your Values: A Guide to Authentic Action
Values are the core principles that define what matters most to you. They serve as your inner compass, guiding decisions, shaping priorities, and giving meaning to your actions. Yet, many of us drift through life without clearly understanding our values, leaving us feeling unanchored or reactive to life's challenges. Identifying and aligning with your values transforms this drift into deliberate action, fostering agency and motivation to pursue what truly matters to you.

Knowing Your Values: A Path to Self-Discovery
Understanding your values is an essential step in getting to know yourself. As Brené Brown aptly puts it, "Living into our values means that we do more than profess our values; we practice them. We walk our talk." Your values reveal your deepest desires—the things that bring you joy, fulfillment, and purpose. For example, if you value honesty, you'll feel most at peace when you act with integrity. If you value connection, cultivating meaningful relationships will be central to your happiness.

Identifying your values gives clarity about what drives you. This self-awareness lays the foundation for making decisions that feel authentic and meaningful. Instead of feeling like life is happening to you, you take an active role in shaping it.

Values as a Source of Agency
Agency—the ability to take intentional, aligned action—is rooted in understanding your values. When you're clear about your values, you no longer feel like a passive participant in your life. You realize you have the power to make choices that reflect your beliefs and priorities.

Simon Sinek's idea of starting with "why" is a great way to think about values. Your why, or your core purpose, provides a grounding force when life feels uncertain or overwhelming. It reminds you of who you are, what you stand for, and what's worth fighting for.

 Try This: Turning Values intto Action Exercise

Knowing your values is just the beginning. The true power of values lies in letting them guide your actions. This alignment fosters integrity and fulfillment, as your daily life begins to reflect what you truly care about.

1. Identify Your Core Values
Take time to reflect on what matters most to you. Consider these questions:

- What brings me joy and fulfillment?
- What principles guide my decisions?
- What would I want others to say about me at the end of my life?

2. Define What Your Values Look Like in Action
Values are most powerful when translated into behaviors.

For instance:
- If you value health, commit to regular movement or balanced nutrition.
- If you value kindness, practice empathy in your interactions.
- If you value growth, take on challenges that stretch your capabilities.

3. Let Your Values Motivate You
When faced with a decision or challenge, pause and ask: "What action aligns with my values?" This simple step helps you avoid reactive or impulsive choices, keeping you focused on what truly matters.

4. Revisit and Reflect on Your Values
As you grow, your values may evolve. Regular reflection ensures that your actions align with who you are becoming.

Values and Motivation in Recovery
In recovery, values act as a powerful motivator, helping you stay aligned with your goals and guiding you toward well-being. Viktor Frankl reminds us in *Man's Search for Meaning* that "Those who have a 'why' to live can bear almost any 'how.'" Living by your values transforms recovery from a burden into a purposeful journey.

For instance:
- If you value connection, you might prioritize building healthy relationships over engaging in harmful behaviors.
- If you value self-respect, you'll likely make choices that nurture your mental and physical health.
- If you value growth, setbacks become opportunities to learn and evolve.

Becoming the Agent of Your Life
When you live by your values, you take ownership of your life. You move beyond external pressures and fleeting emotions, acting with intention and clarity. This sense of agency empowers you to navigate challenges, pursue meaningful goals, and cultivate resilience.

Final Thoughts
Your values are the bridge between who you are and who you want to become. They guide your actions, inspire growth, and remind you of what's possible when you act with integrity. Discovering and living your values isn't just about making better choices—it's about building a life that feels authentically yours.

Take the time to uncover what truly matters to you. Let your values inspire every step forward, anchoring you in a sense of purpose and guiding you toward a life that reflects the best of who you are.

Filling the Void: Replacing Addictive Behaviors with Engagement and Purpose

Addictive behaviors often leave behind a profound void—consuming time, energy, and emotion while offering little in return. When these behaviors are removed, it's common to feel disoriented, as though a significant piece of life is missing. But here's the truth: that space isn't just a void—it's an invitation to transformation.

By reconnecting with what brings you joy and discovering what gives your life meaning, you can fill that space with engagement and purpose. These are not just tools but lifelines, offering new ways to thrive and build a fulfilling life.

Understanding the Void
Let's be honest: addictive behaviors often serve as temporary escapes. They numb pain, distract from discomfort, or mask feelings of emptiness. Removing those behaviors may feel like ripping off a bandage, exposing wounds that are raw and unhealed. But that emptiness? It's not just a loss; it's fertile ground—a blank slate to plant the seeds of a more vibrant, meaningful existence.

Instead of fearing the void, embrace it as a space for growth. What will you build? What passions, pursuits, or values will you allow to take root?

Engagement: The Key to a Fulfilling Life
Engagement is more than just staying busy—it's about immersing yourself in activities that captivate your attention

and bring you into the present moment. As psychologist Mihaly Csikszentmihalyi described, "flow" is a state where challenge and skill align, creating a sense of effortlessness and satisfaction.

In recovery, engagement offers a powerful antidote to the patterns that fuel addictive behaviors. When you focus on meaningful activities, you redirect your energy and attention away from temptations and negative thoughts toward growth and joy.

Steps to Foster Engagement
- **Explore Your Interests**: What hobbies or passions have you neglected? What new experiences are you curious about?

- **Find Flow Activities**: Seek tasks that challenge you in just the right way—creative projects, sports, or even puzzles can be deeply absorbing.

- **Practice Presence**: Bring mindfulness to your activities, focusing on the sensations, emotions, and thoughts they evoke.

Purpose: The Compass That Guides You
Purpose is your why—the reason you get up in the morning. As Viktor Frankl famously observed, "Those who have a 'why' to live can bear almost any 'how.'" Purpose provides clarity, motivation, and resilience, guiding you toward decisions that align with your values and long-term goals.

In recovery, purpose is transformative. It fills the emptiness with a sense of belonging and direction, making life not just about avoiding harm but about pursuing fulfillment.

From Void to Vitality
Here's the thing: engagement and purpose aren't overnight fixes. They're commitments—investments in a life worth living. By replacing destructive behaviors with fulfilling activities and meaningful goals, you reshape the void into vitality.

Start small. Dedicate a few minutes each day to something that excites or inspires you. Over time, these small actions add up, creating a life rich with connection, satisfaction, and growth.

A New Chapter
The space left by addiction isn't the end of the story—it's a blank canvas waiting for your brushstrokes. Engagement and purpose give you the tools to paint a life filled with joy, connection, and meaning.
You don't need to rush. Begin with curiosity, explore what matters to you, and trust the process. Recovery isn't just about letting go of what no longer serves you—it's about building a life that does.

Reinventing Yourself: Living a Purpose-Driven Life
Every day offers a fresh chance to redefine who you are and how you show up in the world. Recovery isn't just about leaving harmful habits behind—it's about stepping into a meaningful, fulfilling life that reflects your deepest values and passions. Reinventing yourself means taking ownership of your story and

replacing isolation and temptation with connection, engagement, and purpose.

The Guiding Light of Purpose

Purpose is your "why"—the force that propels you forward and gives your life direction. Viktor Frankl's work reminds us that when we have a reason to live, we can endure almost any challenge. Purpose shifts your focus from what you're leaving behind—like addictive behaviors—to what you're moving toward: a vibrant, intentional life aligned with your passions and values.

Start with questions like:
- What inspires me and sparks joy?
- Who do I admire, and why?
- How can I contribute in ways that feel meaningful?
- What values do I want to live by?

Filling the Void with Meaningful Engagement

Addictive behaviors often mask an emotional or psychological void. Purpose-driven engagement fills that space with life-affirming activities. When you immerse yourself in experiences that align with your values, you replace destructive habits with meaningful pursuits.

The Science of Purpose and Engagement

Research shows that living with purpose enhances resilience, reduces stress, and rewires the brain for healthier patterns. Purpose-driven activities:

- **Release Healthy Dopamine**: Natural highs from meaningful activities activate the brain's reward system.

- **Build Emotional Resilience**: Purpose buffers against stress, making challenges more manageable.

- **Foster Connection**: Acts of purpose often involve contributing to others, deepening belonging and reducing isolation.

 Try This: Reinventing Yourself Exercise

Reflect on Your Purpose
Explore what truly matters to you. Ask:
- What gives my life meaning?
- When do I feel most alive?
- What values do I want to embody?

Take Purposeful Action
Purpose requires action. Begin with small, intentional steps:
- Volunteer for a cause you care about.
- Revisit hobbies or interests that light you up.
- Set meaningful goals that inspire forward momentum.

Create a Vision for Your Future
Recovery is a blank canvas. Envision who you want to become:
- How do I want to show up in relationships and daily life?
- What legacy do I want to leave behind?

A Purpose-Driven Life Transforms Recovery
Purpose is transformative. It replaces the pull of addictive behaviors with meaningful pursuits and provides resilience during setbacks. By engaging in purposeful activities, you build connection, reduce isolation, and create a foundation for a life full of joy and fulfillment.

Reinventing yourself is not about erasing your past but about building a future aligned with your truest self. Your values and purpose guide you to rediscover your passions, reignite your engagement with life, and embrace the person you're becoming.

You hold the power to choose intentionality, connection, and purpose. Start today—one small, purposeful step at a time—and let the life you're creating reflect the strength, passion, and resilience that lies within you.

The Transformative Power of Acts of Service and Kindness

Purpose doesn't always have to come from grand gestures or monumental achievements. Sometimes, it's as simple as stepping outside your own struggles to support someone else. Acts of service and kindness not only benefit those you help but also strengthen your own recovery journey, creating a ripple effect of positivity and connection.

Engaging in acts of service shifts your focus from what's missing in your life to what you can give. Whether you're volunteering at a community organization, writing a kind note, or offering a listening ear to a friend, these small actions build meaningful connections, reinforce your sense of purpose, and boost your emotional resilience. Science backs this up: studies show that acts of kindness activate the brain's reward system, releasing feel-good chemicals like dopamine and oxytocin, while reducing stress and enhancing mental well-being.

Why Kindness and Service Matter

- **Shift Perspective:** Helping others can make your own challenges feel more manageable, reminding you that you're not alone.

- **Build Connection:** Service fosters relationships and combats isolation, creating a sense of belonging.

- **Create Purpose:** Knowing you've made a difference reinforces your self-worth and commitment to recovery.

- **Boost Resilience:** Acts of kindness lower stress and enhance emotional well-being, helping you better navigate triggers and challenges.

Service as a Recovery Tool
Service replaces destructive habits with meaningful activities, reframing your identity as someone who contributes rather than struggles. Each act of kindness strengthens your recovery journey and reminds you of the power you hold to impact the world around you.

Final Summary

Engagement and purpose are powerful forces in the recovery journey, offering pathways to rediscover joy, creativity, and meaning. Engagement immerses you in activities that energize and fulfill, while purpose provides a guiding light that aligns your actions with your values and aspirations. Together, they replace the void left by addictive behaviors, fostering resilience, reducing temptations, and creating a life rooted in authenticity and growth. By embracing engagement and purpose, you build a framework for living that prioritizes connection, fulfillment, and the pursuit of a meaningful future.

Key Takeaways

Engagement Creates Fulfillment: Engaging in activities that captivate your attention and bring joy helps replace destructive patterns with meaningful experiences. These moments of flow reduce stress, enhance well-being, and reconnect you with creativity and passion.

Purpose Provides Direction: Purpose acts as a compass, guiding your decisions and aligning your life with your core values. It turns recovery from a process of avoidance into a journey of growth and self-discovery.

Fills the Void Left by Addiction: Addictive behaviors often leave a profound gap in your life. Engagement and purpose fill this void with meaningful pursuits, transforming challenges into opportunities for connection and fulfillment.

Builds Resilience: Living with purpose and engaging in valued activities strengthens your ability to navigate setbacks and face challenges with clarity and determination.

Supports Recovery Long-Term: Engagement and purpose provide a sustainable framework for recovery, replacing harmful habits with a life built on authenticity, connection, and meaning.

Engagement and Purpose Pulse Check

Reflecting on your journey with the RECOVERY Sunshine Assessment, take a moment to evaluate your current level of engagement and purpose and how they are shaping your well-being and recovery. Consider this a focused check-in on this essential ray of sunshine, offering insight into where you are and where you can nurture growth.

Ascribe

On a scale of 1–10, how engaged and purposeful do you feel in your daily life? Use these questions to guide your rating:
- How often do you immerse yourself in activities that bring joy and fulfillment?
- Do you feel a sense of direction and meaning guiding your choices?
- Are your actions aligned with your values and long-term goals?
- When faced with challenges, do you feel motivated by a deeper "why"?
- How connected are you to activities, people, or causes that matter most to you?

Describe

Reflect on why you gave yourself that score:
- What recent activities or experiences have made you feel deeply engaged or connected to your purpose?
- Have you felt aligned with your values, or do you notice areas where you've been acting reactively?

- What moments stand out where you felt fully immersed or motivated by something meaningful?
- How have engagement and purpose helped you navigate a difficult situation or avoid harmful habits?

Prescribe
Identify one action you can take to deepen your sense of engagement and purpose:
- What's one activity you've been meaning to explore that could bring joy or fulfillment?
- How can you take a small step toward a goal that aligns with your values?
- What's one way you can connect with a cause or community that resonates with you?

Actionable Inspirations
Here are practical ways to foster engagement and cultivate purpose:
- Dedicate 20 minutes this week to a hobby or passion that lights you up.
- Volunteer for a cause that aligns with your values or interests.
- Reflect on your "why" by journaling about your goals and what motivates you.
- Revisit an activity or skill that brought you joy in the past.
- Have a meaningful conversation with someone who inspires you or shares your values.

Sentence Completions

Deepen your connection to engagement and purpose with these prompts:
- An activity that makes me feel truly alive is…
- One small step I can take toward my purpose is…
- When I feel connected to my values, I notice…
- A cause or community I'd love to contribute to is…
- My "why" that inspires me to keep going is…

Mantra for Engagement and Purpose

"I align my actions with my values, creating a life of joy, meaning, and fulfillment."

Or create your own:

_____

A SPARK of HOPE

Remember, it's not about giant leaps; it's about small, intentional steps that align with who you are and where you want to go. Whether it's diving into a creative project, volunteering for a cause you care about, or simply exploring what makes you feel alive, each choice you make brings you closer to a life of engagement and fulfillment. Your journey is uniquely yours, and every effort you make to embrace your values and find your purpose is a step toward a brighter, more connected future. Trust in your ability to discover what makes your life meaningful—you're already on your way.

CHAPTER 8: ENGAGEMENT AND PURPOSE

What sparked your curiosity or caught your attention?
(Reflect on what you found interesting or intriguing.)
_____
_____
_____
_____

What insights or ideas feel actionable or relevant to your life?
(Identify what you can apply or implement.)
_____
_____
_____
_____

What resonated deeply or felt personally meaningful to you?
(Consider what moved or inspired you emotionally or intellectually.)
_____
_____
_____
_____

CHAPTER 9

Reflection and Mindfulness

Awareness brings clarity and guides action. Sometimes, the most transformative moments in life happen in the quiet spaces—those brief pauses where you tune in to your thoughts, emotions, and the world around you. Reflection and mindfulness are not just practices; they're pathways to clarity, healing, and resilience. In recovery, they become tools for navigating the complexities of triggers, understanding your inner landscape, and making decisions that align with your values. By learning to pause and observe rather than react, you reclaim your power to create a life that feels intentional, grounded, and deeply fulfilling.

REFLECTION AND MINDFULNESS

"Your vision will become clear only when you look into your heart. Who looks outside, dreams; who looks inside, awakens." – Carl Jung

Imagine facing a moment of intense temptation, where the urge feels overwhelming, and instinct seems to take over. Now picture pausing, taking a deep breath, and choosing a path that aligns with your goals and values. This simple yet profound shift—from reacting impulsively to responding intentionally—is the power of reflection and mindfulness in action.

Recovery is a transformative journey that requires both courage and deep self-awareness. Reflection and mindfulness are two foundational practices that illuminate this path, helping you navigate challenges with clarity and intention. These practices are not merely tools to overcome difficulties; they are gateways to a life filled with balance, purpose, and inner peace.

Reflection encourages you to look inward with curiosity and compassion. It allows you to explore your emotions, behaviors, and patterns, providing insight into what drives your actions. By understanding your triggers and setbacks, reflection transforms pain into growth, fostering resilience and hope.

Mindfulness, on the other hand, anchors you in the present moment. It teaches you to observe your thoughts and emotions without judgment, creating the space to respond rather than react. Through mindfulness, you can manage stress, regulate emotions, and maintain clarity even during life's most challenging moments.

By cultivating reflection and mindfulness, you develop the emotional stability and self-awareness necessary to navigate recovery and align your actions with your values. These practices not only enhance your ability to overcome challenges but also empower you to live a more intentional, balanced, and fulfilling life.

Self-Awareness Through Reflection: Understanding Your Feelings, Needs, and Wants

Self-awareness is the cornerstone of personal growth and emotional well-being. Through the power of reflection, we develop the ability to tune into our own feelings, needs, and desires, creating a foundation for making intentional choices that align with our values and goals. Reflection is not just about looking inward; it's about fostering a deeper connection with yourself and understanding what drives your thoughts, emotions, and actions.

Why Self-Awareness Matters
When we take the time to reflect on our feelings, needs, and wants, we gain clarity about what is truly important to us. This awareness helps us identify patterns, both positive and negative, that influence our behavior. For those managing addictive behaviors or seeking recovery, self-awareness becomes a pow-

erful tool to break free from unhealthy coping mechanisms and replace them with intentional, fulfilling actions.

Reflection allows you to:
- **Understand Your Emotions**: Identifying what you're feeling helps you respond thoughtfully rather than reacting impulsively.

- **Clarify Your Needs**: Recognizing what you need enables you to take proactive steps to meet those needs in healthy ways.

- **Articulate Your Desires**: Knowing what you truly want helps you align your actions with your long-term goals and values.

Reflection in Action: A Simple Exercise
One way to cultivate self-awareness is through a brief, reflective exercise. Ask yourself these three questions, either silently, aloud, or in a journal:

What am I feeling right now?
This step helps you name your emotions without judgment, acknowledging their presence as valuable signals.

What am I needing right now?
Identifying your needs helps you connect with what your body, mind, or heart is asking for—whether it's rest, reassurance, connection, or clarity.

What am I wanting right now?
This final question brings focus to your desires and how they align with your goals, empowering you to take meaningful action.

For example:
- If you're feeling overwhelmed, you might realize you need a moment of calm and want to spend 10 minutes meditating.

- If you're feeling lonely, you might identify a need for connection and want to reach out to a friend or loved one.

The Power of Awareness
Self-awareness helps you get your needs met effectively, reducing the likelihood of turning to unhealthy coping mechanisms. By regularly reflecting on your feelings, needs, and wants, you create a practice of checking in with yourself—building emotional resilience, fostering self-compassion, and empowering healthier decisions.

In recovery, this practice can be transformative. Instead of ignoring or suppressing emotions, you learn to understand and address them in ways that support your well-being. Self-awareness becomes the bridge between your inner world and the meaningful, purposeful life you're striving to build.

Reflection is an act of self-care. By pausing to understand what you feel, need, and want, you're honoring your inner experience and paving the way for intentional growth. Take a moment today to check in with yourself—you might be surprised at the clarity and strength you find within.

Mindfulness: Anchoring Yourself in the Present Moment for Recovery

Mindfulness—the practice of being fully present without judgment—is like a reset button for the mind. When life feels overwhelming or temptations creep in, mindfulness offers a way to pause, breathe, and choose your next step with intention. It's not just about "sitting and breathing"; it's about living in the here and now, aware of your emotions, choices, and the power you have to change your trajectory.

The Science of Mindfulness and Recovery
Ever feel like your brain is on autopilot, pulling you into old habits? Mindfulness helps break that cycle. Studies show that mindfulness strengthens the prefrontal cortex—the part of your brain responsible for self-control and decision-making—and quiets the amygdala, the brain's fear and stress center (Hölzel et al., 2011).

In recovery, mindfulness can:

- **Reduce Temptations:** By observing urges as temporary waves, you can detach from the need to act on them.

- **Enhance Emotional Regulation:** Mindfulness teaches you to sit with stress, anger, or sadness without defaulting to harmful coping mechanisms.

- **Increase Self-Awareness:** Being present helps you notice triggers and patterns in behavior, empowering healthier choices.

Mindfulness in Action: Simple Practices for Recovery

Think of mindfulness as a toolbox, with practical strategies you can use in moments of need. Here are three simple yet powerful tools:

The STOP Method
Stop what you're doing, Take a breath, Observe your thoughts and feelings, and Proceed mindfully. Imagine you're at a crossroads—this method helps you pause and choose the path that aligns with your goals.

Body Scan Meditation
Close your eyes and slowly bring your attention to different parts of your body, from your toes to your head. Notice any tension or discomfort without trying to change it. This practice helps ground you in your body and the present moment.

Mindful Breathing
Sometimes all it takes is focusing on your breath to bring you back to center. Try inhaling for four counts, holding for four, and exhaling for four. You'll feel the shift almost instantly.

Mindfulness and Breaking the Cycle of Addiction

Addictive behaviors often arise from a desire to escape discomfort. Mindfulness offers another path: facing those feelings with curiosity and compassion instead of avoidance.

For instance:
- **Managing Temptations:** When an urge arises, mindfulness lets you observe it like a passing cloud, reminding yourself, "This too shall pass."

- **Building Resilience:** Regular mindfulness practice helps you tolerate discomfort, whether it's stress, cravings, or emotional lows.

- **Reclaiming Choice:** Mindfulness creates space between a trigger and your response, giving you the power to make intentional decisions rather than defaulting to old habits.

A Mindful Path to Healing

Recovery isn't about flipping a switch; it's about creating new habits, one mindful moment at a time. Mindfulness is your ally in this process, helping you navigate challenges with clarity and compassion.

Each time you pause to breathe, reflect, or simply notice the world around you, you're not just disrupting harmful patterns—you're building a life filled with awareness and intention. So today, take a moment to ground yourself. Whether it's a deep breath, a quiet walk, or simply noticing the feel of your feet on the floor, these small moments of mindfulness have the power to transform your journey.

Mindfulness: Finding Calm and Balance in the Present Moment

Mindfulness is the practice of being fully present, moment by moment, with openness and non-judgment. It invites you to step away from the mental chatter of past regrets and future anxieties, focusing instead on observing your thoughts, emotions, and sensations as they arise. This practice offers a profound way to manage stress, enhance emotional well-being, and regain control over reactive habits, including addictive behaviors.

The Science of Mindfulness and Stress Management
Mindfulness has a strong foundation in neuroscience and psychology, demonstrating its effectiveness in reducing stress and enhancing resilience. Here's how it works:

- **Activates the Parasympathetic Nervous System**: Mindfulness calms the body's "fight or flight" response, shifting you into a state of rest and recovery (Kabat-Zinn, 1990).

- **Improves Emotional Regulation**: Studies reveal that mindfulness strengthens the prefrontal cortex, the brain's control center for managing emotions and decision-making (Hölzel et al., 2011).

- **Fosters Neuroplasticity**: Regular mindfulness practice rewires the brain, enhancing areas responsible for attention, empathy, and self-regulation.

- **Reduces Negativity Bias**: The brain's natural tendency to dwell on negative experiences is balanced by mindfulness, which cultivates a more positive and constructive outlook.

These changes not only reduce stress but also build resilience, allowing you to face life's challenges with greater calm and clarity.

Mindfulness in Practice: Simple Tools for Anchoring Yourself

Present Moment Awareness
Mindfulness anchors you in the present by focusing on your breath, body, or surroundings. This attention to the here and now interrupts the spiral of stress or overthinking.

Non-Judgmental Observation
Mindfulness teaches you to observe thoughts and emotions without attaching labels like "good" or "bad." This promotes self-acceptance and alleviates the guilt or shame often tied to stress or temptations.

Real-Time Resilience
Mindfulness techniques, such as deep breathing or grounding in your senses (e.g., noticing the texture of an object or the sounds around you), can help you remain calm in moments of high stress.

Mindfulness: A Tool for Stress and Recovery

In today's fast-paced, stress-laden world, mindfulness serves as a vital tool for emotional regulation and resilience. By anchoring yourself in the present, you can disrupt automatic stress responses, engage with challenges constructively, and find calm in the chaos. This practice doesn't erase difficulties but provides a steady foundation from which to approach them.

Mindfulness invites you to breathe, pause, and be—turning each moment into an opportunity for healing and growth. Whether you're managing everyday stress or navigating the complexities of recovery, mindfulness offers a way to meet life with openness, balance, and resilience.

Reflection and Mindfulness: A Powerful Duo for Navigating Triggers and Recovery

When it comes to recovery, reflection and mindfulness are like the dynamic duo of personal growth. Together, they offer tools to navigate life's challenges with clarity and resilience, turning even the toughest moments into opportunities for meaningful change. These practices, foundational to Acceptance and Commitment Therapy (ACT), help you not only understand your triggers but also respond to them in ways that align with your values and goals.

Reflection: Understanding Your Triggers

Think of reflection as pressing pause on your inner dialogue. It's about taking a moment to step back and ask yourself the important questions: "Why did that situation make me feel this way?" or "What am I really seeking right now?" For anyone navigating triggers, this kind of self-inquiry can be a game-changer.

How Reflection Helps with Triggers:
- **Spotting Patterns:** Reflection shines a light on recurring emotions or situations that spark temptations. For instance, are you more likely to feel triggered when you're tired or stressed?

- **Understanding Needs:** Often, what's driving a craving isn't the habit itself but an unmet need, like the desire for comfort or connection. Reflection helps you identify these underlying needs.

- **Fostering Acceptance:** By acknowledging your emotions without judgment, you create space to address them thoughtfully rather than reacting impulsively.

Mindfulness: Staying Grounded in the Present

If reflection is pressing pause, mindfulness is staying in the moment. It's the practice of observing your thoughts and feelings without judgment or the need to act on them. Mindfulness invites you to experience the "here and now," helping you break free from the endless loop of past regrets or future worries.

How Mindfulness Complements Reflection:
- **Breaking the Chain:** Mindfulness interrupts the cycle of reactivity, giving you a chance to choose your response instead of defaulting to old patterns.

- **Managing Emotions:** When things get overwhelming, mindfulness helps you stay calm and grounded, reducing the emotional highs and lows that often lead to impulsive actions.

- **Building Self-Compassion:** Observing your thoughts without judgment cultivates kindness toward yourself, a key ingredient in navigating recovery.

The Role of ACT: Acceptance and Commitment Therapy

ACT encourages embracing your thoughts and feelings instead of fighting them, helping you align your actions with your core values. Reflection and mindfulness fit beautifully within this framework by promoting acceptance, defusion, and committed action.

Key Elements of ACT in Reflection and Mindfulness:
- **Acceptance:** Both practices teach you to accept your emotions as they are rather than suppressing or avoiding them.

- **Defusion:** Mindfulness helps you see thoughts as just thoughts—not facts—allowing you to let go of unhelpful mental narratives.

- **Committed Action:** Reflection transforms insights into intentional actions that align with your values and support your recovery.

Example: Navigating a Trigger with Reflection and Mindfulness
Imagine this: You're feeling a strong urge to give in to a familiar habit during a stressful moment. Mindfulness steps in first, encouraging you to pause and notice what's happening. What does this urge feel like in your body? What thoughts are swirling in your mind? Then comes reflection: What might this urge be signaling? Are you feeling lonely, overwhelmed, or exhausted?

With this awareness, you now have the power to respond intentionally—perhaps by taking a walk, journaling, or reaching out to a supportive friend—rather than reacting impulsively.

Integrating Reflection and Mindfulness into Recovery
To harness the combined power of reflection and mindfulness:

1. **Start with Awareness:** Ground yourself in the present moment with mindfulness. Observe your thoughts and feelings without rushing to judge or act on them.

2. **Reflect on Patterns:** Once the moment has passed, ask yourself: What triggered this reaction? What need might I have been trying to meet?

3. **Act with Intention:** Use your insights to guide meaningful actions that align with your recovery goals and values.

Reflection and mindfulness are not about achieving perfection—they're about building awareness and intention, one moment at a time. These practices help you move from reacting to responding, empowering you to face triggers with clarity and confidence. Recovery is a journey, and with reflection and mindfulness as your guides, each step becomes an opportunity for growth and healing.

Decoupling Thought from Action: Thoughts Are Not Commands

Our minds generate thousands of thoughts daily—some helpful, others intrusive or distressing. In recovery, it's crucial to recognize that not every thought demands action. This concept, known as decoupling thought from action, is a key principle in mindfulness and self-reflection, empowering you to regain control over your choices.

Understanding the Nature of Thoughts
Thoughts are natural mental events, not direct instructions. They often reflect fleeting emotions, past experiences, or automatic reactions. By learning to observe thoughts without judgment, you can create space between what you think and how you act. This pause allows you to respond intentionally rather than react impulsively.

How Self-Reflection Helps
Self-reflection enables you to examine your thoughts with curiosity and compassion. Ask yourself:

- Where is this thought coming from?
- Is it based on facts or assumptions?
- Does acting on this thought align with my values and goals?

By reflecting on your thoughts, you can challenge their validity and choose a course of action that supports your recovery and well-being.

The Role of Mindfulness
Mindfulness teaches you to observe your thoughts as they arise, without becoming entangled in them. Practices like mindful breathing or grounding techniques help you stay anchored in the present, reducing the power of intrusive thoughts. Over time, mindfulness strengthens your ability to let thoughts pass like clouds in the sky—acknowledged but not acted upon.

Example: Reclaiming Control
Imagine experiencing a temptation or urge to engage in an addictive behavior. Instead of acting immediately, you pause, take a deep breath, and notice the thought. You might think, "I need this to feel better," but through mindfulness, you recognize it as just a thought, not a command. Self-reflection helps you align your response with your recovery goals, choosing an action that nurtures your long-term well-being.

Building Resilience Through Decoupling
Decoupling thought from action empowers you to act intentionally rather than impulsively. It reduces stress, strengthens emotional regulation, and reinforces the belief that you are not controlled by your thoughts. With practice, reflection, and

mindfulness, you'll find that your thoughts become guides rather than rulers, helping you make choices that align with your values and recovery.

Take a moment today to notice your thoughts, acknowledge them without judgment, and remind yourself: **Thoughts are not commands—they're just thoughts.**

Reflection and Mindfulness: Responding Instead of Reacting

In the heat of the moment, triggers—whether stemming from stress, emotional pain, or temptations—can lead to impulsive reactions that may not align with your values or recovery goals. Reflection and mindfulness offer an alternative: the ability to pause, process, and respond thoughtfully instead of reacting impulsively.

The Traffic Signal Metaphor: Responding vs. Reacting
Think of your mind as a traffic signal:
- **Red Light (Reacting):** Reacting is like running a red light—impulsive, immediate, and often risky. It bypasses deliberate thought and is driven by automatic responses like anger, fear, or temptation.

- **Green Light (Responding):** Responding is like waiting for the green light—mindful, intentional, and aligned with your values. It allows you to pause, process, and act with awareness.

Mindfulness and reflection work together to help you stop at the red light, pause, and wait for the green light, empowering you to make choices that support your well-being and long-term goals.

Mindfulness: The Pause Button for Your Mind

Mindfulness is the practice of bringing your attention to the present moment without judgment. It creates a mental space to observe your thoughts, feelings, and physical sensations, giving you the clarity to process triggers before acting on them.

- **Processing Triggers:** Mindfulness allows you to notice triggers as they are—emotional or physical sensations—without labeling them as good or bad.

- **Regulating Emotions:** It calms the nervous system, reducing emotional overwhelm and helping you think clearly.

- **Creating Awareness:** Mindfulness helps you recognize the patterns behind your reactions, offering a chance to break unhealthy cycles.

Reflection: Turning Awareness into Action

Reflection complements mindfulness by encouraging you to delve deeper into your experiences and understand their roots. While mindfulness focuses on the present, reflection helps you explore the "why" behind your feelings and triggers, guiding you toward thoughtful responses.

- **Identify Patterns:** Reflection helps uncover recurring triggers and their connection to your thoughts and emotions.

- **Align with Values:** It allows you to ask, "Does this behavior align with who I want to be?"

- **Plan for the Future:** Reflection helps you create strategies for handling similar situations in healthier ways.

▶ **Try This: Reflection and Mindfulness Exercise**

Imagine a situation where a trigger arises—a temptation or an emotional challenge. Mindfulness creates the initial pause, allowing you to observe the experience without judgment. Reflection follows as you consider your needs and values, empowering you to choose a response that aligns with your goals.

Example: Practicing the Green Light Approach Emma, in recovery from social media overuse, often found herself endlessly scrolling when stressed. Through mindfulness, she began noticing her trigger—a sense of loneliness—and pausing before reacting. Reflection helped her identify her need for connection. Instead of reaching for her phone, Emma chose to call a friend, fulfilling her need in a healthier way.

Steps to Practice the Green Light Approach
1. **Pause:** When you feel triggered, take a few deep breaths to ground yourself.

2. **Reflect:** Ask yourself, "What am I feeling? What am I needing? What am I wanting?"

3. **Choose:** Decide on a response that aligns with your values and recovery goals.

Building a Mindful, Reflective Recovery
By combining the grounding power of mindfulness with the insights of reflection, you can create space between a trigger and your response—a space where growth and empowerment thrive. This practice not only helps you manage triggers but also deepens your connection to yourself, supporting a recovery journey grounded in clarity, resilience, and purpose.

Urge Surfing: Riding the Wave of Temptations

Temptations can feel overwhelming, demanding immediate action and making us believe they are impossible to resist. However, mindfulness-based techniques like urge surfing, developed by Dr. Alan Marlatt, offer a transformative approach to managing urges. This practice empowers you to ride out temptations by observing them as temporary experiences that naturally rise, peak, and subside—just like a wave.

What Is Urge Surfing?

Urge surfing, rooted in **mindfulness-based relapse prevention (MBRP)**, invites you to face temptations without suppression or impulsive reaction. Instead of being controlled by your urges, you become an observer of your internal experience. By acknowledging the sensations in your body and emotions in your mind, you remind yourself that urges are not commands—they are fleeting experiences that pass with time (Marlatt & Gordon, 1985).

The Role of Reflection and Mindfulness

Reflection and mindfulness work hand in hand to support urge surfing. Mindfulness anchors you in the present moment, helping you notice and accept urges without judgment or panic. Meanwhile, reflection helps you recognize patterns in your behavior and prepare for future temptations. Together, they provide tools to manage triggers with clarity and composure.

When practicing urge surfing, you might ask yourself:

- **What am I feeling right now?** Identify the emotions or sensations associated with the temptation.

- **What is this urge trying to fulfill?** Acknowledge the underlying need, whether it's for comfort, connection, or relief from stress.

- **How can I respond in alignment with my recovery goals?** Choose an action that supports your long-term well-being.

▶ Try This: Urge Surfing Exercise

1. **Acknowledge the Temptation:**
   When an urge arises, name it without judgment. Say to yourself, "This is a temptation. It will pass."

2. **Breathe Deeply:**
   Use slow, deep breaths to center yourself. Mindful breathing calms the nervous system and creates a moment of pause (Hölzel et al., 2011).

3. **Observe the Sensations:**
   Notice the physical sensations of the urge. Is it a tightness in your chest? Restlessness in your hands? Simply observe without trying to change it.

4. **Visualize the Wave:**
   Picture the urge as a wave. Watch as it rises, peaks, and eventually fades. Remind yourself that no wave lasts forever.

5. **Reflect After the Urge Passes:**
   Once the temptation subsides, take a moment to reflect. What helped you ride it out? How can you use this experience to build resilience for the future?

The Benefits of Urge Surfing
Urge surfing not only helps you manage temptations but also strengthens self-regulation and emotional resilience. Research shows that mindfulness enhances self-control by engaging the prefrontal cortex and calming the amygdala, reducing the

emotional intensity of triggers (Hölzel et al., 2011; Baer, 2003). Over time, this practice diminishes the power of urges and helps you feel more in control of your actions.

Why It Works:
Reduces Reactivity: Urge surfing creates a pause between the trigger and your response, giving you the space to choose healthier alternatives.

Reclaims Agency: By observing rather than reacting, you remind yourself that you have control over your choices.

Fosters Resilience: Each time you ride out an urge, you build confidence in your ability to handle discomfort and stay committed to your recovery.

A Mindful Path Forward
Recovery is a journey, and urges are part of the process. With urge surfing, you can face temptations with curiosity and composure, transforming them from obstacles into opportunities for growth. By integrating mindfulness and reflection into your daily routine, you strengthen your ability to navigate challenges and stay aligned with your goals.

Take a moment today to practice urge surfing. The next time a wave of temptation arises, remind yourself: "I can ride this wave. It will pass." Each wave you surf brings you closer to a life of intention, balance, and resilience.

Mindfulness-Based Stress Reduction (MBSR): A Pathway to Recovery and Resilience

Recovery is a journey of understanding and transformation, and **Mindfulness-Based Stress Reduction (MBSR)** offers a practical, research-backed method to support that journey. Developed by Dr. Jon Kabat-Zinn in the 1970s, MBSR combines mindfulness practices like body scans, mindful movement, and meditation to help individuals manage stress, regulate emotions, and navigate life's challenges. For those recovering from addictive behaviors, it provides tools to reconnect with the present moment, break free from reactive patterns, and foster long-term resilience.

Why MBSR Is a Game-Changer for Recovery
Addictive behaviors often arise as attempts to escape discomfort, numb emotional pain, or cope with overwhelming stress. MBSR tackles these underlying drivers by creating space between triggers and responses, reducing stress, and cultivating self-awareness.

- **Breaking Reactive Patterns**
  MBSR helps you pause and observe triggers without automatically reacting. This creates space to make choices that align with your recovery goals, breaking the cycle of addiction.

- **Reducing Stress**
  Chronic stress fuels temptations. MBSR activates the parasympathetic nervous system (the "rest and digest" mode), calming the mind and body (Hölzel et al., 2011).

- **Enhancing Emotional Regulation**
  By strengthening the prefrontal cortex—the brain's center for thoughtful decision-making—MBSR improves your ability to manage emotions and navigate triggers (Hölzel et al., 2011).

- **Encouraging Self-Compassion**
  Shame and guilt can be barriers to recovery. MBSR fosters kindness toward yourself, helping you approach your journey with acceptance rather than criticism.

- **Promoting Neuroplasticity**
  Regular mindfulness practice rewires the brain, forming healthier neural pathways that support resilience and recovery (Bowen et al., 2014).

The Science Behind MBSR
Research consistently highlights the effectiveness of MBSR in supporting recovery:

- A study in *Substance Abuse* found that mindfulness-based programs significantly reduced substance use and cravings, helping participants build healthier habits (Bowen et al., 2014).

- MBSR has been shown to lower cortisol levels, the stress hormone linked to triggering addictive behaviors (Hölzel et al., 2011).

- Mindfulness decreases rumination and strengthens emotional regulation, critical factors in managing the ups and downs of recovery.

How MBSR Addresses Addictive Behaviors
Awareness of Triggers
MBSR teaches nonjudgmental awareness, helping you recognize triggers as they arise and observe them without feeling controlled by them.

Tolerance of Discomfort
Practices like the body scan allow you to sit with uncomfortable sensations or emotions without escaping into harmful behaviors.

Breaking Temptation Cycles
By cultivating mindfulness, you can interrupt automatic reactions and reflect on whether acting on urges aligns with your long-term goals.

Building Resilience
MBSR enhances your ability to face challenges with clarity, equipping you to handle setbacks and emotional turbulence.

Try This: Mindfulness Based Stress Reduction Exercise

While attending a formal MBSR program is beneficial, you can start incorporating its practices into your daily life:

Body Scan Meditation

Lie down or sit comfortably. Bring your attention to different parts of your body, noticing sensations without judgment. This practice connects you to your physical self and reduces stress.

Mindful Breathing

Focus on the natural flow of your breath. When your mind wanders, gently guide it back. This anchors you in the present and calms the nervous system.

Sitting Meditation

Sit comfortably and observe your thoughts and emotions as they arise, letting them pass without attachment. This practice builds self-awareness and emotional regulation.

Mindful Movement

Engage in yoga or gentle stretching, focusing on the sensations of each movement. This practice strengthens the connection between mind and body.

Everyday Mindfulness

Bring mindfulness into daily activities like eating, walking, or conversations:

- **Eating:** Savor each bite, noticing the flavors, textures, and smells.

- **Walking:** Pay attention to the sensation of your feet on the ground and the rhythm of your breath.

- **Listening:** Fully focus on the words, tone, and body language of the person you're speaking with.

A Mindful Path to Healing

MBSR is not just a stress-relief tool—it's a transformative practice that helps you address the root causes of addictive behaviors. By cultivating awareness, reducing stress, and fostering emotional resilience, MBSR empowers you to navigate recovery with clarity and strength.

Even small steps toward mindfulness can create profound shifts. Consider starting today—whether by focusing on your breath, observing your thoughts, or simply pausing to notice the present moment. Each mindful act brings you closer to a life rooted in peace, balance, and purpose.

Healing Trauma and Finding Meaning Through Your Hero's Journey

Trauma leaves marks—not just on the mind but on the body as well. These imprints shape how we see the world and interact with it. Recovery, however, isn't about erasing the pain. It's about transforming it into something meaningful and empowering, just like the heroes in our favorite stories. By integrating mindfulness, reflection, and somatic healing, you can chart your own path to resilience and growth.

Mindfulness: Listening to Your Body and Mind

Mindfulness invites you to press pause and tune into the present moment. As Dr. Bessel van der Kolk highlights in *The Body*

Keeps the Score, trauma often shows up as tension or discomfort stored in the body. Mindfulness-based practices like body scans and gentle movement can help release these sensations, reconnecting you to a sense of safety. Think of mindfulness as a way to ask your body, "What are you holding onto, and how can I help you let go?"

Reflection: Discovering Strength in Your Story
Reflection builds on mindfulness by helping you uncover the lessons hidden in your pain. Instead of seeing trauma as something that breaks you, reflection reframes it as part of your hero's journey. Joseph Campbell's concept of the hero's path reminds us that every great story begins with a challenge. By asking questions like, "What has this experience taught me?" or "How has it shaped my values?" you begin to see your pain as a stepping stone to becoming your most authentic self.

Somatic Healing: Releasing Pain Stored in the Body
Trauma doesn't just live in the mind—it's etched into the body, too. Practices like yoga, mindful movement, and breathwork act as bridges between physical sensations and emotional release. For example, mindful stretching or a body scan meditation can help you gently "unpack" areas of tension, offering your body the release it's been longing for.

The Hero's Journey: From Pain to Purpose
Every challenge holds the seeds of transformation. Joseph Campbell's hero's journey teaches us that setbacks are not the end—they're the turning point. Mindfulness helps you approach painful memories with curiosity, while reflection allows you to weave these moments into a meaningful narrative. Instead

of seeing trauma as a period, it becomes a comma—part of a longer, richer story about resilience and growth.

▶ Try This: Hero's Journey Exercise

- **Mindful Reflection:** Spend 10 minutes journaling about what you're feeling, needing, or wanting. Let these reflections guide your actions.

- **Body Scan Meditation:** Lie down or sit comfortably, and slowly bring your attention to different parts of your body. Notice where you hold tension and breathe into those areas.

- **Hero's Story Journaling:** Write about a challenging experience and explore how it shaped your values or strengths. What lessons have you taken forward?

Becoming the Hero of Your Story
Recovery is your chance to rewrite the narrative of your life. Mindfulness and reflection aren't just tools for healing—they're keys to transforming pain into purpose. Your story is still unfolding, and every moment of self-awareness brings you closer to the hero you're meant to be. So pause, reflect, and step forward with courage. The best chapters are yet to come.

Final Summary

Reflection and mindfulness form a powerful duo in the recovery journey, offering tools to build awareness, resilience, and emotional balance. Through mindfulness, you anchor yourself in the present moment, creating space to observe thoughts, emotions, and triggers without judgment. Reflection complements this by helping you process those experiences, uncover patterns, and align your actions with your values. Together, these practices empower you to respond thoughtfully rather than react impulsively, fostering growth and intentionality in your recovery.

By embracing mindfulness and reflection, you cultivate clarity, compassion, and self-awareness—essential elements for navigating challenges and fostering meaningful change. These practices help you not only manage triggers and temptations but also deepen your connection to yourself and the life you are building. Recovery is not just about overcoming difficulties; it's about creating a future filled with purpose, resilience, and peace.

Key Takeaways

Reflection Cultivates Self-Awareness
Reflection helps you identify patterns in your thoughts, emotions, and behaviors, offering clarity about triggers, needs, and desires. This awareness empowers you to make choices that align with your values and recovery goals.

Mindfulness Anchors You in the Present
Mindfulness creates a pause between triggers and reactions, allowing you to observe your experiences without judgment. This practice fosters emotional regulation and helps you respond thoughtfully rather than impulsively.

Combining Reflection and Mindfulness Enhances Growth
When paired, reflection and mindfulness offer a holistic approach to recovery. Mindfulness grounds you in the present, while reflection provides insight into past experiences, helping you navigate challenges with intention and resilience.

Mindfulness Calms the Nervous System
By engaging practices like mindful breathing and body scans, you activate the parasympathetic nervous system, reducing stress and promoting emotional balance.

Reflection Guides Intentional Action
Through reflection, you align your actions with your long-term goals and values, transforming insights into meaningful steps forward in your recovery.

You Can Respond Instead of Reacting
The practice of mindfulness and reflection creates a "green light" pause, empowering you to make intentional, value-driven choices instead of reacting impulsively to triggers.

Integration Is Key to Sustainable Recovery
Incorporating daily moments of mindfulness and regular reflection strengthens your resilience, deepens self-compassion, and fosters long-term growth in your recovery journey.

 **Reflection and Mindfulness Pulse Check**

Reflecting on your journey with the RECOVERY Sunshine Assessment, take a moment to evaluate your current level of mindfulness and self-awareness and how they are shaping your well-being and recovery. Consider this a focused check-in on these essential rays of sunshine, offering insight into where you are and where you can grow.

Ascribe
On a scale of 1–10, how present are mindfulness and reflection in your daily life? Use these questions to guide your rating:
- How often do you take time to reflect on your thoughts, feelings, and actions?
- Are you intentional about pausing and observing your emotions and triggers without judgment?
- Do you use mindfulness practices, such as deep breathing or meditation, to stay grounded?
- How often do you create space for self-awareness and thoughtful decision-making?
- Are you able to respond thoughtfully to triggers instead of reacting impulsively?

Describe
Reflect on why you gave yourself that score:
- What recent practices or habits have helped you build mindfulness or self-awareness?
- Have there been moments where you struggled to reflect or pause before reacting?

- What emotions or triggers have been most challenging, and how have you managed them?
- In what ways has mindfulness or reflection positively impacted your recovery or well-being?
- What stands out as a moment where mindfulness or self-awareness helped you navigate a tough situation?

Prescribe

Identify one action you can take to deepen your practice of reflection and mindfulness:
- What's one small mindfulness practice, like mindful breathing or a short meditation, that you can integrate into your day?
- How can you create a habit of daily reflection, such as journaling or reviewing your day?
- What's one trigger you can prepare for by practicing mindfulness or reflection ahead of time?
- How can you remind yourself to pause and observe when faced with a challenge?

Actionable Inspirations

Here are practical ways to cultivate mindfulness and reflection:
- Start a daily journaling practice, asking yourself: "What am I feeling? What am I needing? What am I wanting?"
- Set a reminder to take three deep, intentional breaths during moments of stress.
- Dedicate five minutes at the end of your day to reflect on what went well and what you learned.
- Practice the STOP method: Stop, Take a breath, Observe, Proceed mindfully.

- Spend a few moments in nature, practicing mindful observation of your surroundings.

Sentence Completions

Deepen your awareness of mindfulness and reflection with these prompts:
- A moment I felt grounded and present today was...
- When I reflect on my emotions, I notice that I...
- To deepen my mindfulness practice, I will...
- One way I can create space for reflection this week is...
- Mindfulness helps me feel...

Mantra for Reflection and Mindfulness

"I honor my journey by pausing, observing, and responding with clarity and purpose."

Or create your own:

_____

_____

_____

A SPARK of HOPE

You hold the power to navigate life's challenges with grace and purpose. Through reflection and mindfulness, you are learning to face each moment with curiosity and compassion rather than fear or avoidance. These practices remind you that you are not defined by your triggers or emotions—you are defined by how you choose to respond. Keep building this connection to yourself. With every pause, every breath, and every thoughtful action, you're reinforcing the foundation of your recovery and stepping into a life filled with clarity, resilience, and possibility.

What sparked your curiosity or caught your attention?
(Reflect on what you found interesting or intriguing.)

_____
_____
_____
_____

What insights or ideas feel actionable or relevant to your life?
(Identify what you can apply or implement.)

_____
_____
_____
_____

What resonated deeply or felt personally meaningful to you?
(Consider what moved or inspired you emotionally or intellectually.)

_____
_____
_____
_____

CHAPTER 10

You-Focused Empowerment

The power to change rests in your hands. You-Focused Empowerment is about stepping into the driver's seat of your life, recognizing that you hold the power to shape your growth, choices, and future. It's not about perfection or having all the answers—it's about cultivating self-awareness, embracing curiosity, and building habits that align with your values. Empowerment is an ongoing process of learning, adapting, and showing up for yourself with courage and intention. In this chapter, we'll explore how fostering intellectual well-being, setting meaningful goals, and connecting with mentors or role models can create a solid foundation for growth and resilience.

YOU-FOCUSED EMPOWERMENT

"Empowerment is the process of becoming stronger and more confident, especially in controlling your life and claiming your rights." — Anonymous

Empowerment begins with you. It's about reclaiming your agency, embracing your strengths, and intentionally designing a life aligned with your values. In recovery, empowerment is not just about breaking free from addictive behaviors—it's about rediscovering your potential, setting meaningful goals, and building a future rooted in growth, purpose, and resilience.

You-focused empowerment shifts the spotlight inward, making you the driving force behind your transformation. By cultivating self-awareness, taking purposeful action, and committing to continuous personal development, you unlock the confidence to navigate challenges and align your life with what truly matters.

This chapter explores intellectual well-being as a cornerstone of empowerment. It's not confined to formal education but thrives in curiosity, lifelong learning, and the joy of discovery. Whether mastering a new skill, diving into a passion, or gaining insight into yourself, nurturing your intellectual well-being fuels resilience and fulfillment. It's this journey of exploration and growth that empowers you to become the architect of a life that reflects your strengths, values, and aspirations.

Empowerment isn't handed to you; it's created by you. When you invest in your potential, embrace curiosity, and commit to growth, you claim the power to shape a purposeful, accomplished, and fulfilling life. This chapter will show you how to take that step forward.

What Is You-Focused Empowerment?

You-focused empowerment is about reclaiming your agency and becoming the agent of your life. It's a mindset and practice that centers on recognizing your potential, celebrating your achievements, and continuously nurturing personal growth. This process fosters intellectual well-being, strengthens self-efficacy, and helps you build a life rooted in purpose and resilience.

The Science Behind You-Focused Empowerment

Achievement and Self-Efficacy

Psychologist Albert Bandura's concept of **self-efficacy** emphasizes the belief in one's ability to influence events and outcomes. When you set and accomplish goals—no matter how small—you reinforce your belief in your capability. This creates a cycle of confidence and motivation that drives further growth.

Research shows that achievement activates the brain's reward system, releasing dopamine, a neurotransmitter associated with pleasure and motivation. This natural boost reinforces positive behaviors and fuels the desire to continue striving toward your goals.

Intellectual Well-Being and Growth

Intellectual well-being is nurtured when we actively seek learning, exploration, and new experiences. The act of mastering a new skill, solving a challenging problem, or engaging in meaningful conversation stimulates neuroplasticity, the brain's ability to form new neural connections. This growth-oriented mindset enhances cognitive resilience and supports recovery by providing fulfilling and constructive ways to spend your energy.

Carol Dweck's research on **growth mindset** highlights the power of viewing challenges as opportunities for development. Adopting this perspective allows you to embrace setbacks as part of the process, helping you stay motivated and engaged in your personal journey.

Purpose and Resilience

Purpose-driven living is closely tied to empowerment. Studies show that individuals with a clear sense of purpose experience lower stress levels, greater resilience, and higher overall satisfaction in life. Connecting your actions to a larger "why" adds meaning to your accomplishments, helping you navigate obstacles with strength and clarity.

How to Cultivate You-Focused Empowerment

Reclaim Your Agency

Recognize that you have the power to influence your life. Start by setting small, actionable goals and celebrating your progress. For example, completing a task you've been putting off can reignite your sense of capability.

Engage in Lifelong Learning
Explore new interests, take up a hobby, or commit to learning something new. Whether it's reading a book, attending a workshop, or mastering a skill, intellectual growth keeps your mind sharp and engaged.

Practice Self-Reflection
Take time to reflect on your achievements, both big and small. Journaling about your progress or revisiting past successes can boost your confidence and reinforce your belief in your potential.

Align with Your Purpose
Connect your goals to your values and long-term aspirations. When you see how your actions contribute to something meaningful, you'll stay motivated and resilient in the face of challenges.

Foster Resilience Through Growth
Use setbacks as opportunities to learn and grow. Remember, every failure is a stepping stone toward success. Cultivating a growth mindset ensures that you view challenges as temporary hurdles rather than insurmountable barriers.

Why You-Focused Empowerment Matters

You-focused empowerment is transformative because it shifts the focus inward, helping you build a life that aligns with your values and aspirations. It encourages self-sufficiency, intellectual growth, and resilience—key components of recovery and well-being. By reclaiming your role as the agent of your life, you create a foundation of accomplishment and purpose that supports your long-term goals.

Empowerment isn't about perfection or competition; it's about recognizing your unique potential and taking intentional steps to nurture it. Each small action you take reinforces your belief in yourself, helping you cultivate a fulfilling, purpose-driven life.

The Role of Intellectual Well-Being in Empowerment and Recovery

When was the last time you felt truly inspired or excited to learn something new? Intellectual well-being—though often overlooked—is a cornerstone of empowerment and recovery. It's not just about degrees or formal education; it's about staying curious, exploring new ideas, and engaging in lifelong learning. When you stimulate your mind, you cultivate resilience, build confidence, and open doors to personal fulfillment.

Why Intellectual Well-Being Matters

Have you ever noticed how energized you feel after solving a tricky puzzle or diving into an engaging book? That's your brain's reward system kicking in. Activities that challenge your mind release dopamine, the same feel-good neurotransmitter often exploited by addictive behaviors. But here's the beauty: intellectual pursuits provide that dopamine boost in a healthy, constructive way.

Research by Ryff and Keyes (1995) shows that intellectual engagement enhances cognitive flexibility, emotional resilience, and overall well-being. In recovery, this translates to a greater ability to adapt to challenges, think creatively about solutions, and maintain a positive outlook on life. Stimulating your mind isn't just enjoyable—it's a tool for transformation.

Intellectual Well-Being in Action
Consider Maria, who found herself struggling with idle time during her recovery. Instead of falling into old patterns, she decided to explore photography. The process of learning new techniques and creating art not only kept her engaged but also gave her a renewed sense of purpose. Each photo she captured became a symbol of her growth and her commitment to a healthier, more fulfilling life.

 Try This: Intellectual Well-Being Exercise

1. **Explore New Interests:** What's something you've always wanted to try? Maybe it's baking, astronomy, or learning the guitar. Engaging in hobbies sparks curiosity and keeps your mind active.

2. **Challenge Your Mind:** Tackle a crossword puzzle, try learning a new language, or start a DIY project that requires problem-solving. These activities strengthen your brain and boost creativity.

3. **Commit to Lifelong Learning:** Whether it's attending a workshop, listening to an inspiring podcast, or simply having meaningful conversations, view every day as a chance to grow and evolve.

Intellectual well-being is about more than keeping your mind busy—it's about enriching your life and rediscovering joy in learning. By staying curious and open to new experiences, you not only empower yourself but also strengthen the foundation of your recovery. This commitment to growth helps you align your actions with your values, paving the way for a purposeful and fulfilling journey.

Building Self-Worth Through Accomplishment

Think about a time when you set a goal and achieved it. Maybe it was something small, like organizing your space, or something bigger, like completing a challenging project. How did that accomplishment make you feel? Accomplishment is a powerful way to build self-worth because it reminds you of your capabilities and strengthens your belief in your ability to overcome challenges. By celebrating each success—no matter the size—you create a positive feedback loop that fuels confidence and resilience.

The Science Behind Accomplishment
Psychologist Albert Bandura's concept of self-efficacy sheds light on why accomplishments matter. When you believe in your ability to influence outcomes, you're more motivated to take action and persevere through obstacles. This belief isn't just theoretical—it directly enhances well-being and resilience.

James Clear, in *Atomic Habits*, offers another layer by introducing identity-based habits. He explains that aligning your actions with the person you want to become reinforces a positive self-image. For example, if you aspire to be disciplined, each small act of discipline—like sticking to a schedule or saying no to distractions—strengthens your belief that you are that person. These small wins build self-worth over time.

Accomplishment in Action
Take Liam's story, for instance. During his recovery, Liam set a goal to run a 5K. At first, it seemed daunting, but each training session became a reminder of his commitment to health and well-being. Crossing the finish line wasn't just a physical achievement—it was proof of his resilience and growth. That sense of accomplishment became a cornerstone of his recovery, inspiring him to take on new challenges with confidence.

How to Build Accomplishment Into Your Life
- **Start Small:** Choose goals that feel achievable right now. Success breeds success, so small wins are key to building momentum.

- **Celebrate Progress:** Recognize each step forward, whether it's finishing a book, making a healthy meal, or taking a walk. Acknowledge the effort you put in, not just the outcome.

- **Align with Your Identity:** Ask yourself, "What would the best version of me do today?" Then take one small action that reflects that identity.

- **Focus on Growth:** See setbacks as part of the process. Every stumble is an opportunity to learn and adjust, not a reason to stop trying.

The Role of Accomplishment in Recovery

In recovery, accomplishment is a powerful antidote to feelings of helplessness or doubt. By setting and achieving meaningful goals, you remind yourself of your ability to grow, adapt, and succeed. Each step forward becomes a testament to your strength and a building block for your self-worth.

Remember, accomplishments don't have to be monumental to matter. Even the smallest steps—making your bed, taking care of your body, or learning something new—are victories worth celebrating. Over time, these moments of progress add up, transforming your sense of self and empowering you to take on life's challenges with confidence.

Continuous Learning and Sustainable Satisfaction

In a world often dominated by instant gratification, continuous learning offers a deeper, more enduring sense of satisfaction. Unlike quick, fleeting highs, the process of learning fosters personal growth, mastery, and fulfillment—key ingredients for long-term happiness and resilience.

The Science of Sustainable Satisfaction

Curiosity, a driver of continuous learning, is strongly linked to increased life satisfaction and emotional resilience. When you stay open to new experiences, you create opportunities for joy, discovery, and self-expansion. This aligns with research from positive psychology, which emphasizes the importance of building on personal strengths. Leveraging these strengths not only amplifies your accomplishments but also reinforces habits that boost confidence and well-being (Seligman, 2011).

Additionally, learning stimulates the brain's reward pathways in a healthy and sustainable way, releasing dopamine—the neurotransmitter associated with pleasure and motivation. This stands in stark contrast to addictive behaviors, which provide short-lived dopamine spikes but ultimately deplete long-term satisfaction.

Why Learning Matters in Recovery
Continuous learning can help make addictive behaviors less apealing, replacing instant gratification with meaningful growth. Each new skill, discovery, or accomplishment builds a sense of mastery, empowering you to take on challenges with confidence and optimism. By investing in lifelong learning, you nurture a foundation of lasting satisfaction that promotes resilience and happiness in recovery and beyond.

Mentorship, Inspiration, and Role Models: Reimagining Yourself

Who lights the spark of possibility in your life? Who inspires you to dream bigger or take the next bold step? Mentors and role models offer more than just admiration—they provide a vision of what's possible and empower us to reimagine our potential. Whether through a personal connection or simply observing someone from afar, the people who inspire us become guides for growth, transformation, and self-discovery.

The Power of Role Models
Role models show us what's achievable by living examples of the qualities or successes we aspire to. According to Albert Bandura's social learning theory, we grow by observing others. Seeing someone overcome challenges or succeed in areas we value reinforces the belief that we can do the same. Role models make abstract dreams feel tangible and accessible.

Consider the "act as if" principle: by emulating the habits or attitudes of someone you admire, you begin to embody those traits yourself. Want to be more confident, disciplined, or creative? Act as if you already are, and you'll strengthen those qualities in real-time. Dr. Ellen Langer's research even shows that adopting a mindset as if something is true can create measurable shifts in your growth and well-being (Langer, 1981).

The Role of Mentorship
Mentorship takes inspiration a step further, providing personalized guidance, encouragement, and accountability. A good mentor doesn't just tell you what to do—they challenge you to think bigger, see new possibilities, and believe in your potential.

Through shared wisdom and lived experience, mentors offer insights that can save you time and frustration on your journey. They become trusted allies, guiding you to take risks, navigate obstacles, and celebrate wins. For many, having a mentor is the key to turning ambition into action and potential into achievement.

Choosing Your Inspirations
In today's connected world, inspiration is everywhere—you just have to look for it intentionally. Take a moment to reflect:

- **Who do you admire?** Think about individuals whose values or accomplishments resonate deeply with you.

- **What sparks envy?** Envy often highlights areas of growth or desires you wish to fulfill.

- **Who leaves you in awe?** Awe points to traits or achievements aligned with your deeper aspirations.

Even your social media feed can be curated for growth. Follow people who inspire you, challenge you to think differently, and embody the person you want to become.

The Science of Inspiration and Growth
Surrounding yourself with mentors and role models bolsters your self-efficacy—the belief that you can achieve your goals (Bandura, 1977). This belief fuels resilience and motivation, helping you push through setbacks and stay focused.

Research also highlights the value of mentorship in reducing stress, building confidence, and accelerating growth. Role models and mentors influence how we see ourselves, shaping the way we engage with challenges and opportunities alike.

▶ **Try This: Reimagining Yourself Exercise**

Role models and mentors don't just inspire us—they give us the courage to reimagine who we can be. Start small:

- Identify one trait or habit from someone you admire.

- Begin practicing the "act as if" principle to bring that quality into your daily life.
- Seek out mentors who can guide you in specific areas of growth or change.

Reinvention doesn't happen overnight—it begins with a spark of inspiration and small, intentional steps. Whether it's a mentor's advice, a role model's example, or your own vision for the future, you have the power to reshape your story and pursue the life you want. The possibilities are endless when you let mentorship and inspiration fuel your growth.

Harnessing Character Strengths: A Pathway to Empowerment

Each of us possesses unique strengths that, when recognized and nurtured, can become transformative tools for personal growth and empowerment. Character strengths are the positive traits inherent to who we are—our natural abilities to think, feel, and act in ways that foster well-being and connection. By harnessing these strengths, we cultivate confidence, resilience, and a deeper sense of fulfillment.

The Science of Strengths
Positive psychology research, spearheaded by Christopher Peterson and Martin Seligman (2004), emphasizes the importance of identifying and using strengths as a pathway to well-being. When you leverage your strengths in daily life:

- **You experience greater flow:** This state of deep engagement arises when your abilities align with meaningful challenges, enhancing satisfaction and achievement.

- **You reinforce resilience:** Focusing on what you're naturally good at boosts self-efficacy and helps you navigate setbacks.

- **You align with purpose:** Using your strengths connects you to activities and causes that resonate with your values.

Putting Strengths Into Action

Maria discovered her top strength was kindness. To embrace this strength, she began volunteering at a local animal shelter. This allowed her to live in alignment with her values, fostering a profound sense of purpose and fulfillment. Whether it's creativity, leadership, curiosity, or love, finding opportunities to use your strengths creates a ripple effect of positivity in your life.

▶ **Try This: Harness Your Strengths Exercise**

1. **Identify Your Strengths:** Tools like the VIA Character Strengths Survey can help you pinpoint your unique traits.

2. **Integrate Strengths into Daily Life:** Look for opportunities to use your strengths in small ways—at work, in relationships, or through hobbies.

3. **Focus on Strength-Based Goals:** Align your goals with your top strengths to amplify motivation and achievement.

By leaning into your natural abilities, you create a foundation of confidence and resilience, empowering you to overcome challenges and live a life of purpose and joy. Harnessing your character strengths isn't just about what you do—it's about who you become.

Act As If: Building Empowering Habits for Recovery and Growth

What if you could begin transforming your life today, simply by acting as if you were already the person you aspire to be? This powerful concept, rooted in Ellen Langer's groundbreaking research on mindfulness and psychology, emphasizes how adopting the behaviors and attitudes of your desired self can lead to profound and lasting change. For those in recovery, acting "as if" becomes a pathway to reshape habits, rebuild self-worth, and step confidently into a new identity.

The Science of Acting "As If"
Ellen Langer's research demonstrates that our actions don't just reflect who we are—they shape who we become. By embodying the traits of the person you want to be, you engage neural pathways that reinforce those behaviors, making them feel more natural over time.

This idea aligns with James Clear's concept of identity-based habits from *Atomic Habits*. Small, intentional actions—like choosing a glass of water in the morning as part of "I value my health"—lay the groundwork for larger transformations, turning goals into realities by first shifting how you see yourself.

Recovery Through Empowering Action
Addictive behaviors often tie individuals to a narrative of struggle or shame. Acting "as if" offers an escape from this narrative, allowing you to embrace a new story centered on empowerment and positive change. Instead of waiting for confidence, resilience, or creativity to magically appear, you step into those roles by practicing them daily.

 Try This: Act "As If" Exercise

- **Define Your Identity:** Who do you want to become? Is it someone who values health, creativity, connection, or resilience?

- **Start with One Habit:** Choose a small, meaningful action that reflects this identity:
    - Want to be an artist? Spend 10 minutes sketching daily.
    - Want to build resilience? Practice mindfulness when stressed.
    - Want to be healthier? Go for an evening walk.

- **Reinforce with Consistency:** Each time you act "as if," you reinforce the neural connections that make your new identity feel real.

A Metaphor for Transformation
Think of acting "as if" like putting on the uniform of your future self. At first, it might feel like you're playing a role, but with time, the uniform becomes a natural fit. This practice bridges

the gap between who you are and who you wish to be, creating space for growth and empowerment.

Liam's Journey
Take Liam, for example. In recovery from addictive behaviors, he dreamed of becoming a writer but doubted his ability. Acting as if he were already a writer, Liam committed to journaling for 10 minutes daily. Over time, this small habit transformed his self-perception and gave him a new sense of purpose, proving that consistent, intentional actions can redefine identity.

The Path to Growth
"Acting as if" isn't about pretending—it's about stepping into possibility. It aligns your actions with your aspirations, creating a future shaped by intention and belief. In recovery, this practice provides an anchor, helping you navigate challenges, rebuild confidence, and embrace new possibilities.

Start today: Who do you want to become? What small action can you take to align with that vision? Begin acting "as if," and watch as your future self unfolds.

Identity-Based Habits: Replacing Destructive Patterns with Purposeful Actions

Identity-based habits, introduced by James Clear in *Atomic Habits*, offer a powerful approach to personal transformation by aligning daily actions with the person you aspire to become. This approach shifts the focus from merely achieving goals to building an empowering sense of identity, which helps replace destructive patterns, foster accomplishment, and promote continuous learning.

The Role of Identity in Transformation
Destructive patterns, such as addictive behaviors, often stem from a disconnect between actions and personal values. Identity-based habits provide a framework to rebuild this connection. By acting in alignment with your desired identity—such as "I am someone who prioritizes my health" or "I am someone who values learning"—you create a foundation for meaningful, lasting change. Each aligned action reinforces this identity, making it easier to stay committed over time.

How Identity-Based Habits Replace Destructive Patterns
1. **Create Positive Momentum:** Small, consistent habits tied to identity build confidence and momentum. For example, replacing the urge to engage in harmful behaviors with a positive action—like journaling or walking—signals a shift toward a healthier self.

2. **Shift from Avoidance to Action:** Instead of focusing on avoiding destructive behaviors, identity-based habits encourage proactive, value-driven behaviors. This approach reduces the internal conflict often associated with change.

3. **Strengthen Resilience:** Acting "as if" you are already the person you want to be (e.g., a creative individual or a resilient person) builds resilience, confidence, and hope. Over time, these habits reshape self-perception and neural pathways, making positive choices feel more natural.

Replacing Destructive Patterns with Identity-Based Habits: An Example

Maria struggled with smoking and wanted to quit. Instead of focusing on "not being a smoker," she reframed her identity: "I am someone who values clean air and vitality." Each time she resisted the urge to smoke, she reinforced this identity. She replaced the habit with deep breathing exercises, which not only aligned with her new self-perception but also reduced her temptations and built resilience.

Why It Works
- **Neuroplasticity:** Repeated actions aligned with identity strengthen neural pathways, helping replace old habits with new, healthier ones.

- **Intrinsic Motivation:** When actions align with identity, motivation comes from within, making habits more sustainable.

- **Emotional Alignment:** Identity-based habits reduce the internal struggle by focusing on who you are becoming rather than what you are avoiding.

Building Your Identity-Based Habits
- **Define Your Desired Identity:** Ask yourself, "Who do I want to become?" Be specific and tie this identity to your values.

- **Start Small:** Identify one habit that aligns with this identity and commit to it daily.

- **Celebrate Small Wins:** Every time you take an action aligned with your identity, acknowledge the accomplishment. Each small step is a victory.

By replacing destructive patterns with identity-based habits, you can rebuild your life with purpose, accomplishment, and continuous learning. This approach not only transforms behavior but also empowers you to become the person you truly want to be.

Curiosity and Novelty: Embracing Life's Excitement and Growth

"Better to try and fail than never to try at all." This simple yet profound idea captures the heart of curiosity—a driving force that makes life vibrant, engaging, and filled with discovery. Curiosity pushes us to explore the unknown, sparking empowerment and igniting a sense of fulfillment. For those navigating recovery or seeking freedom from addictive behaviors, embracing curiosity can reawaken a passion for life and cultivate resilience.

The Science Behind Curiosity and Novelty

Curiosity is a core human trait that fuels learning and exploration. Studies show that encountering new experiences activates the brain's reward system, releasing dopamine—a neurotransmitter associated with pleasure and motivation. This same system, often hijacked by addictive behaviors, can be rewired by pursuing positive, novel activities.

Novelty keeps your brain alert and engaged, preventing emotional and mental stagnation. Research highlights that trying new things promotes cognitive flexibility, enhances emotional well-being, and creates a sense of accomplishment. Life becomes an adventure, full of fresh possibilities, leaving little room for destructive patterns.

The Joy of Play and Exploration
Curiosity thrives on play, trial, and discovery. In *The Power of Play*, Elaine O'Brien and I discuss how playful exploration fosters joy, creativity, and connection. Play isn't just for children—it's a state of mind that invites experimentation, courage, and growth.

Trying something new, whether it's picking up a hobby, learning a skill, or stepping into an unfamiliar experience, is an act of bravery. It's about embracing imperfection and learning along the way, which in turn empowers you to grow and expand your world.

How Curiosity and Novelty Empower You
- **Break the Routine:** Curiosity disrupts monotony, encouraging you to step out of your comfort zone and explore healthier, meaningful alternatives.

- **Build Confidence:** Every new endeavor—whether successful or not—reinforces your ability to adapt, persevere, and thrive.

- **Enhance Resilience:** Novel experiences teach you to embrace uncertainty and handle challenges with creativity and strength.

- **Reignite Joy:** Exploring something new rekindles excitement for life, providing a powerful buffer against stress and temptations.

Transforming Addictive Behaviors Through Curiosity
Addictive behaviors often promise excitement or escape, but they deliver neither in the long term. Curiosity offers a sustainable and fulfilling alternative. Immersing yourself in novel activities—whether it's trying a new sport, picking up an instrument, or experimenting in the kitchen—creates genuine engagement and purpose.

Take Mark's story, for example. Early in his recovery, Mark felt consumed by boredom and a sense of emptiness. A friend suggested he try paddleboarding. Though hesitant, Mark gave it a shot. He found the experience exhilarating, challenging, and rewarding. The joy of being outdoors and trying something new gave him a sense of freedom and accomplishment that transformed his outlook.

▶ **Try This: Spark Curiosity Exercise**

- **Ask Questions:** What interests you? What's something you've always wanted to try but never did?

- **Explore the Unfamiliar:** Visit a new café, explore a different neighborhood, or attend a class that intrigues you.

- **Set Small Challenges:** Commit to learning one new thing a week—whether it's a recipe, a yoga pose, or a random fun fact.

- **Practice Non-Judgment:** Let go of the fear of failure. View each attempt as an opportunity to grow, regardless of the outcome.

Curiosity is the antidote to monotony and a powerful tool for growth. It invites you to live with wonder, replacing destructive habits with meaningful exploration and discovery. Life isn't about avoiding failure—it's about showing up, trying, and growing with every step.

So, what are you curious about today? Start small, stay open, and let curiosity guide you toward a more vibrant, fulfilling life.

Shifting Focus from Pain to Purpose: Growing and Learning Through Struggles

Life's challenges can leave us feeling defeated, but empowerment lies in how we choose to respond. Rather than allowing pain to define us, we can use it as a catalyst for growth and transformation. By shifting focus from pain to purpose, struggles become stepping stones to a stronger, more meaningful life.

The Science of Growth Through Adversity

Research on post-traumatic growth (Tedeschi & Calhoun, 2004) highlights that adversity, when processed and reframed, can lead to:

- **A Deeper Appreciation for Life:** Challenges clarify what truly matters, encouraging us to prioritize joy and connection.

- **Stronger Relationships:** Facing hardship deepens bonds through shared vulnerability and support.

- **A Renewed Sense of Purpose:** Struggles often spark a re-evaluation of values, guiding us toward meaningful action.

By reflecting on pain and connecting it to personal growth, individuals can foster resilience and reduce the likelihood of relapse. Empowerment comes from seeing struggles not as setbacks, but as opportunities to cultivate strength and purpose.

Finding Purpose in Pain
Pain, though difficult, can become a motivator for meaningful change. Embracing struggles as part of your unique story fosters resilience and helps align actions with your values. Transforming hardship into a foundation for hope propels you toward a life filled with purpose and fulfillment.

Process Emotions Through Writing: Empowering Yourself Through Reflection
Writing is a transformative tool for self-empowerment, offering clarity, emotional release, and a pathway to growth. Psychologist James Pennebaker's research shows that expressive writing improves mental health, enhances emotional clarity, and helps individuals make sense of adversity. Writing provides a deeply personal way to process emotions, foster resilience, and reclaim your story.

Writing as a Tool for Empowerment
By putting pen to paper, you access emotions and insights that may feel inaccessible in daily life. Writing offers a safe space to:

- Process emotions such as shame, guilt, or fear, fostering self-compassion.

- Identify your needs, values, and triggers, deepening self-awareness.

- Reframe challenges as opportunities for growth, cultivating a mindset of empowerment.

In recovery, writing bridges the gap between emotions and understanding, helping you shift focus from setbacks to personal growth.

 Try This: Power of Writing Exercise

Stream of Consciousness Writing: Spend 10–15 minutes writing freely, allowing your thoughts and feelings to flow without structure or judgment. This uncovers emotions and patterns you may not notice otherwise.

Focused Journaling Prompts: Reflect intentionally on questions such as:

- What am I feeling right now, and why?
- What actions align with my values today?
- How can I use this moment to grow?

Reframing Challenges: Rewrite a difficult experience with a focus on the strengths you gained and the lessons you learned. This practice reinforces your ability to grow from adversity.

Example:
Liam, navigating recovery and self-doubt, used journaling to reflect on his challenges. Through writing, he identified moments where he had overcome difficulties in the past, reframing his current struggles as opportunities for resilience and growth.

From Pain to Empowerment: The Power of Reflection and Purpose
Empowerment isn't about avoiding pain—it's about using it as a foundation for growth. Through reflection and writing, you can transform adversity into a narrative of resilience and self-discovery. Pain becomes a teacher, and writing becomes your tool for processing, understanding, and thriving.

Take time today to reflect and write. By intentionally engaging with your emotions and aligning your actions with purpose, you reclaim your power and step boldly into a life filled with meaning and fulfillment. Remember, you are not just overcoming struggles—you are creating a new, empowered story, one word at a time.

Envisioning Your Future Self: Empowerment Through Achievement and Growth

Imagining your future self is a transformative exercise in personal empowerment. By creating a clear, inspiring vision of who you want to become, you unlock motivation, resilience, and purpose. Positive psychology offers practical tools to not only visualize this future version of yourself but also take actionable steps to bridge the gap between where you are now and where you want to be.

The Power of Vision
Visualizing your future self taps into intrinsic motivation and provides clarity for your actions. Dr. Laura King's research (2001) demonstrates that imagining your "best possible self" enhances mood, boosts resilience, and fosters goal-oriented behavior. This isn't just about wishing for success—it's about focusing on the steps that lead you there, empowering you to take consistent, purposeful actions.

Crafting Your Future Self

Start With Self-Reflection
Ask yourself:

- Who do I want to be in one year, five years, or ten years?
- What values, habits, and skills define my future self?
- How will my future self feel, act, and contribute to the world?

Use Positive Psychology Interventions
- **Best Possible Self Exercise:** Write about your future self in detail, focusing on your achievements, character traits, and relationships.

- **Strength-Based Planning:** Identify your top strengths and consider how they can support your vision.

Envision the Process, Not Just the Outcome
Psychologist Gabrielle Oettingen's WOOP method (Wish, Outcome, Obstacle, Plan) provides a structured approach:

1. **Wish:** Define your aspiration (e.g., "I want to complete a professional certification").

2. **Outcome:** Visualize the positive impact of achieving it.

3. **Obstacle:** Anticipate challenges (e.g., "I might procrastinate").

4. **Plan:** Create strategies to overcome obstacles (e.g., "I will schedule study sessions").

Learning and Growing Along the Way
The journey to becoming your future self is as important as the destination. Every challenge is an opportunity to build skills, confidence, and resilience. By focusing on small, consistent actions, you create momentum and cultivate a growth mindset.

Example: A Vision in Action
Maria envisioned herself as a confident public speaker. She didn't stop at imagining a TED Talk; she broke her goal into achievable steps:

- Joining a Toastmasters group.
- Practicing speeches with friends.
- Watching and analyzing great presentations for inspiration.

With each small step, Maria not only improved her skills but also grew into the version of herself she aspired to be.

Your future self isn't a far-off dream—it's built through daily actions. By visualizing who you want to become and taking small, intentional steps, you align with your highest potential. Begin today: close your eyes and imagine your future self. Then, take one action—no matter how small—that brings you closer to that vision. Each step is a powerful testament to your commitment to growth, learning, and empowerment.

Building Empowering Habits: Structuring Your Path to Success

Habits shape your daily life and ultimately define your future. Now that you've envisioned your future self, drawn inspiration from mentors, and committed to prioritizing you-focused empowerment, it's time to take actionable steps. Building empowering habits that align with your vision and values creates a framework for sustained growth and self-development.

Habits are the building blocks of empowerment. By integrating intentional routines into your life, you reinforce your goals and foster a sense of accomplishment. Developing these habits allows you to take control of your journey, boosting your confidence and belief in your ability to succeed.

The Role of Empowering Habits
Empowering habits connect your daily actions to your long-term aspirations. These small, consistent behaviors keep you grounded and focused, ensuring that every step you take aligns with your vision. Research by Charles Duhigg, author of *The Power of Habit*, emphasizes that habits automate behaviors, making it easier to sustain progress over time.

Habits are particularly valuable in recovery, providing structure and replacing destructive patterns with positive, growth-oriented practices. Whether it's exercising to support mental health or journaling to process emotions, habits become your tools for navigating challenges and building a fulfilling life.

How to Build Empowering Habits

Start With Keystone Habits
Keystone habits are transformative routines that have a ripple effect on other areas of your life. For instance, exercising regularly not only boosts physical health but also improves mood, energy, and focus. Journaling can enhance emotional clarity and goal-setting, leading to better decision-making throughout the day.

Use Habit Stacking
Build new habits by linking them to existing ones. This method, popularized by James Clear in *Atomic Habits*, leverages your current routines as anchors for new behaviors.

- Meditate for a few minutes after brushing your teeth.
- Take three deep breaths at a red light to reset your focus.
- Listen to a motivational podcast while folding laundry.

Track Your Progress
Monitoring your habits helps build momentum and reinforces your commitment. Use a journal, app, or checklist to track daily, weekly, and even monthly habits. Celebrate your consistency, no matter how small the achievement.

Example in Practice
Sarah, focused on reclaiming her life after recovery, created an empowering evening routine. She began journaling each night to reflect on her progress and set intentions for the next day. This simple habit helped her end each day on a positive note, strengthened her sense of control, and aligned her actions with her long-term goals. Over time, her confidence grew, and she felt more connected to her vision for the future.

The Transformative Power of Habits
Building empowering habits is more than just creating routines—it's about crafting a life that reflects your goals and values. These habits provide a sense of accomplishment, keep you moving toward your aspirations, and offer stability during times of uncertainty.

By starting small and staying consistent, you can transform your daily actions into a source of confidence and empowerment. Each habit reinforces your belief in your ability to create meaningful change, supporting not only your recovery but also your overall well-being.

Take control of your life, one habit at a time. Write your habits down, track your progress, and celebrate your growth. Empowerment begins with the small, intentional steps you take every day.

Final Summary

You-focused empowerment is the practice of reclaiming your agency and becoming the architect of your growth and transformation. It emphasizes self-awareness, purposeful habits, and intellectual well-being as essential tools for creating a fulfilling and resilient life. By understanding your values, setting meaningful goals, and embracing curiosity, you build a solid foundation for sustainable recovery and joy.

Empowerment is not a one-time milestone but an ongoing process of aligning your actions with your aspirations. Through identity-based habits and continuous learning, you overcome obstacles and evolve into the best version of yourself. This journey is about more than recovery—it's about thriving, unlocking your potential, and fully embracing the life you are capable of creating.

······················ **Key Takeaways** ······················

Reclaim Your Agency
Empowerment begins with taking ownership of your choices, actions, and growth.

Align Actions With Aspirations
Purposeful habits and intentional actions help bridge the gap between where you are and where you want to be.

Embrace Curiosity and Learning
Exploring new interests and committing to lifelong learning fosters resilience and personal growth.

Focus on Identity-Based Habits
Small, consistent actions that reflect who you want to become build self-efficacy and confidence over time.

Empowerment Is an Ongoing Process
Growth doesn't stop with achieving recovery—it continues as you align with your values, set meaningful goals, and pursue a thriving, fulfilling life.

Celebrate Your Progress
Recognize and honor every step forward, no matter how small. Each accomplishment reinforces your resilience and potential.

 ## You-Focused Empowerment Pulse Check

Reflecting on your journey with the RECOVERY Sunshine Assessment, take a moment to evaluate your current level of empowerment and personal growth and how they are shaping your well-being and recovery. Consider this a focused check-in on this essential ray of sunshine, offering insight into where you are and where you can foster resilience and self-discovery.

Ascribe
On a scale of 1–10, how empowered and growth-oriented do you feel in your daily life? Use these questions to guide your rating:
- How often do you take intentional actions that align with your goals and values?
- Do you feel confident in your ability to overcome challenges and adapt?
- Are you engaging in activities that promote learning and self-improvement?
- How often do you embrace curiosity or explore new opportunities for growth?
- Do you feel a sense of agency and ownership over your choices and progress?

Describe
Reflect on why you gave yourself that score:
- What recent actions or choices have made you feel empowered or proud of your progress?
- Are there areas where you've felt reactive or unsure, and how might you address them?

- What moments stand out where you embraced a challenge or learned something new?
- How has focusing on empowerment and personal growth helped you navigate a tough situation?

Prescribe

Identify one action you can take to strengthen your sense of empowerment and foster growth:
- What's one habit or skill you've been meaning to develop that could build confidence?
- How can you take a small step toward a goal that stretches you in a meaningful way?
- What's one way you can channel curiosity into exploring something new or exciting?

Actionable Inspirations

Here are practical ways to nurture you-focused empowerment and growth:
- Commit to learning something new this week, whether it's through a book, podcast, or class.
- Set a small, achievable goal and celebrate your progress as you work toward it.
- Reflect on your strengths by writing down three qualities that help you succeed.
- Step outside your comfort zone by trying an unfamiliar activity or skill.
- Spend time with a mentor or role model who inspires you to grow.

Sentence Completions
Deepen your connection to you-focused empowerment with these prompts:
- A habit or skill I'd like to develop is…
- A recent action that made me feel proud of myself was…
- When I take ownership of my choices, I feel…
- To stretch myself this week, I will…
- I feel most empowered when I…

Mantra for You-Focused Empowerment
"I take intentional steps toward my goals, building resilience, confidence, and joy in the process."

Or create your own:
_____
_____
_____

A SPARK of HOPE

Empowerment isn't about waiting for the right moment—it's about creating it. Each step you take toward growth, no matter how small, is a testament to your strength and commitment to yourself. You don't have to have all the answers today; you simply need to start. Embrace curiosity, lean into learning, and trust that every choice aligned with your values brings you closer to the life you're building. Remember, the journey of empowerment isn't linear—it's a dynamic process of discovery, resilience, and transformation. You are capable, and you are worthy. Keep going—you've got this.

What sparked your curiosity or caught your attention?
(Reflect on what you found interesting or intriguing.)

_____
_____
_____
_____

What insights or ideas feel actionable or relevant to your life?
(Identify what you can apply or implement.)

_____
_____
_____
_____

What resonated deeply or felt personally meaningful to you?
(Consider what moved or inspired you emotionally or intellectually.)

_____
_____
_____
_____

PART 3

BRINGING RECOVERY TO LIFE

*"The best way to predict your future
is to create it."*

– Abraham Lincoln

CHAPTER 11

Building Your Recovery Blueprint: Illuminating the Path Forward

There is a difference between wanting change and living it every day. Real change is built in the small moments, in the decisions made when no one is watching, in the commitment to your future self. Lasting change is born not from willpower alone, but from waypower—the clear, intentional steps you take to bring your vision to life. This is about crafting a daily blueprint, a path that reminds you of the life you're choosing to build. Every action, every decision, is a chance to reaffirm your commitment to yourself and the life you want. This is the journey of integrating recovery into who you are, making it part of the fabric of your days.

BUILDING YOUR RECOVERY

"Your life does not get better by chance;
it gets better by change." – Jim Rohn

Recovery begins with self-awareness and clarity. Before building lasting habits, it's essential to pause, take stock of where you are, and clarify where you want to go. **The RECOVERY Sunshine Assessment** becomes a compass for this process, offering a snapshot of your strengths and areas for growth while helping you transform reflection into inspired action.

Creating your **recovery blueprint** means crafting a personalized map—a tool to guide intentional steps that align with your values and aspirations. There is a difference between wanting change and living it every day. Real change is built in the small moments, in the decisions made when no one is watching, in the commitment to your future self. Lasting change is born not from willpower alone, but from **waypower**—the clear, intentional steps you take to bring your vision to life. This is about crafting a daily blueprint, a path that reminds you of the life you're choosing to build. Every action, every decision, is a chance to reaffirm your commitment to yourself and the life you want. This is the journey of integrating recovery into who you are, making it part of the fabric of your days.

Recovery isn't just about leaving behind what no longer serves you; it's about designing a life that feels authentic, fulfilling, and whole. Let's use the power of self-awareness, small intentional steps, and inspired action to illuminate your path and create a roadmap for lasting transformation.

Hope Theory & Waypower: Foundation for Transformation

Recovery is built on more than a desire to change—it requires both the motivation to take the first step and the tools to keep going. This is where **hope theory** shines as a powerful framework for transformation. Developed by psychologist C.R. Snyder, hope theory shows us that lasting change emerges from the combination of **willpower** and **waypower**.

What is Hope Theory?
At its core, hope theory defines hope as the dynamic interplay between:

- **Willpower**: The inner drive and determination to pursue a goal.
- **Waypower**: The ability to identify actionable steps and strategies to overcome obstacles and achieve that goal.

Hope isn't wishful thinking—it's a practical, grounded approach to transformation. In recovery, hope fuels your belief that change is possible and gives you the tools to make it happen.

The Role of Willpower
Willpower is the engine that drives your recovery journey. It's the motivation that gets you started and keeps you moving forward, even in the face of challenges. However, willpower alone has its limits. Like a muscle, it can become fatigued if overused without support.

For example:
- Relying solely on willpower to avoid temptations can feel exhausting.
- Without a clear roadmap, even the strongest determination can falter.

The Power of Waypower
Waypower transforms willpower into sustainable action by providing clarity and direction. It's the roadmap that helps you navigate obstacles and stay on track, ensuring your recovery journey is not just driven by determination but also guided by intentional planning.

Waypower involves:
- Breaking goals into small, achievable steps.
- Identifying practical strategies to overcome challenges.
- Celebrating progress to build momentum.

With waypower, you can approach recovery with confidence, knowing you have a clear path forward.

Why Waypower Matters
Without waypower, even the strongest willpower can falter. Imagine having the desire to reach a destination but no directions to get there. Waypower fills that gap, offering the tools and strategies needed to turn intention into action.

Waypower in Action:
- **Navigating Obstacles**: When setbacks arise, waypower helps you see challenges as problems with solutions, not insurmountable barriers.

- **Building Confidence**: Each step taken with waypower fosters a sense of agency and belief in your ability to succeed.

- **Creating a Sustainable Plan**: Waypower equips you to craft a recovery blueprint tailored to your strengths, values, and goals.

Hope as the Synergy of Willpower and Waypower

Hope emerges when willpower and waypower work together:

- Willpower says, **"I can do this."**
- Waypower adds, **"Here's how I'll make it happen."**

This synergy creates a sense of empowerment and direction, transforming recovery into a process of intentional growth. Instead of feeling stuck or overwhelmed, you'll have the tools to take consistent, meaningful steps toward the life you want to build.

By combining the motivation of willpower with the actionable strategies of waypower, you cultivate hope—the foundation for lasting transformation. With these tools in hand, recovery becomes not just a possibility but a pathway to a life filled with purpose, balance, and fulfillment.

RECOVERY Sunshine Assessment: A Tool for Clarity and Action

The RECOVERY Sunshine Assessment offers a starting point for crafting your recovery blueprint. This tool invites you to visualize your well-being as a radiant sun, with each RECOVERY principle representing a ray of light. The **RECOVERY Sunshine Assessment** is a resource you've encountered earlier in this book, designed to provide insight into your well-being and recovery journey. Now, as you craft your Recovery Blueprint, it's the perfect time to revisit this tool.

Revisiting Your Sunshine

Recovery is not static—it evolves with time, experience, and growth. By retaking the **RECOVERY Sunshine Assessment**, you gain an updated snapshot of where you are today and where you might want to focus your energy moving forward. Whether you're revisiting your earlier results or taking the assessment for the first time, this is an opportunity to reflect on your progress and recalibrate your journey.

Reflect on Your Results:
- Which rays shine the brightest? Celebrate these strengths.
- Which rays feel dim? Identify opportunities for growth.

How to Use Your Sunshine Results
1. **Reassess and Realign**: Use your sunshine results to pinpoint areas where you're shining brightly and where more light is needed. Identify which RECOVERY principles align most closely with your current goals.

2. **Create a Growth Plan**: Based on your updated sunshine diagram, select one or two principles to focus on. Break your goals into small, actionable steps that align with your values.

3. **Celebrate Your Progress**: Take time to honor the areas where you've grown. Every brightened ray is a testament to your resilience and intentional action.

Quick Tip for Accessibility
If you haven't already taken the **RECOVERY Sunshine Assessment** or need a refresher, you can download or revisit it by visiting **www.readyforrecovery.life**. This resource remains available for ongoing reflection and support throughout your journey.

Inspired Action From Reflection
Your Recovery Blueprint starts with clarity, and the sunshine tool is a compass that helps you navigate the path ahead. Let its insights guide your inspired actions, empowering you to make meaningful, lasting changes that reflect the life you're building. Whether you're nurturing strengths or illuminating dim areas, each step brings you closer to a life of balance, fulfillment, and joy.

Set Focus Areas and Goals
Use your sunshine assessment to prioritize the principles you want to nurture. This isn't about fixing everything at once—it's about taking small, meaningful steps.

Examples of Focus Areas:
- If **Empathy and Self-Compassion** feels dim: Commit to practicing self-kindness by replacing self-criticism with affirmations.

- If **Vitality and Health** needs attention: Aim to take a 10-minute walk each afternoon.

Minimum Viable Interventions (MVIs): Small Steps, Big Impact

In his book *Small Changes, Big Results*, Tal Ben-Shahar highlights the transformative power of small, consistent actions. These actions, referred to as Minimum Viable Interventions (MVIs), are the simplest steps you can take to create meaningful and lasting change. By focusing on what is manageable and achievable, MVIs allow you to build momentum without feeling overwhelmed.

What Are Minimum Viable Interventions?
MVIs are small, deliberate actions designed to bridge the gap between where you are now and where you want to be. These interventions are "minimum" because they focus on the smallest, most manageable step forward, and "viable" because they are realistic and capable of producing meaningful results over time.

Rather than striving for perfection or monumental shifts, MVIs encourage progress through incremental growth. When applied consistently, these small steps compound, creating significant transformation in your recovery and well-being.

Using MVIs to Take Action on the RECOVERY Principles
The RECOVERY principles provide a framework for identifying areas of focus. MVIs bring these principles to life by offering actionable steps you can take to illuminate areas that feel dim or need nurturing. Here are examples of MVIs for each principle:

R: Resilience and Growth *MVI*: Write down one challenge you've overcome each day and reflect on the strength it required.

E: Empathy and Self-Compassion *MVI*: Replace one self-critical thought with a supportive affirmation, such as, "I'm doing the best I can."

C: Connection and Positive Relationships *MVI*: Reach out to a friend or loved one and schedule a phone call or coffee date to reconnect.

O: Optimism and Gratitude *MVI*: Each evening, list three things you're grateful for, no matter how small.

V: Vitality and Health *MVI*: Take a 10-minute walk outdoors or swap a sugary snack for a piece of fruit.

E: Engagement and Purpose *MVI*: Spend five minutes each day working on a project or activity that lights you up.

R: Reflection and Mindfulness *MVI*: Dedicate two minutes each morning to mindful breathing or set a daily intention.

Y: You-Focused Empowerment *MVI*: Acknowledge one personal strength or small win each day and celebrate it.

Creating Your Waypower Goals
MVIs are not just isolated actions; they are part of a broader strategy rooted in **waypower**, as discussed earlier. With your RECOVERY Sunshine Assessment as a guide, you can create actionable goals for the areas you'd like to improve. Here's how to do it:

1. **Identify Your Focus Areas**: Revisit your Sunshine Assessment to see where you want to shine brighter.

2. **Set Specific MVIs**: Choose small, tangible actions for each area of focus.

3. **Track Your Progress**: Use a journal or habit tracker to monitor your actions and reflect on their impact.

4. **Adjust as Needed**: Revisit your goals and MVIs periodically, refining them to stay aligned with your evolving recovery journey.

The Power of Small Changes
The science of neuroplasticity shows that small, repeated actions can rewire the brain, replacing old patterns with new, healthier ones. Tal Ben-Shahar's research underscores that small changes—like MVIs—are not just effective but essential for sustain-

able growth. These actions require less willpower and reduce the risk of burnout, making them ideal for building lasting habits.

A Journey of Celebration and Growth

As you integrate MVIs into your daily life, remember to celebrate your progress. Each small step forward is a victory, a reflection of your commitment to growth and well-being. Over time, these actions will illuminate your path, helping you build a life filled with purpose, joy, and resilience.

Inspired Action: Aligning With Who You Want to Be

In the pursuit of personal growth and recovery, every choice you make matters. Inspired action goes beyond habits or routines; it's about deliberately choosing behaviors that align with the person you aspire to be. It's about living in harmony with your values and goals—not by chance, but with intentionality and purpose.

What Is Intentional Action?

Intentional action is rooted in mindfulness and purposeful decision-making. Instead of reacting to triggers or emotions automatically, it requires a moment of pause, reflection, and a deliberate choice about your next step. Over time, these small, intentional steps build momentum, strengthen self-belief, and foster meaningful change.

Inspired action and intentional action are intertwined. Acting with intention ensures your daily choices align with your vision, creating a bridge between who you are now and who you want to become.

Defining Who You Want to Be
At the heart of inspired action lies a pivotal question: **Who do I want to be?**

Reflect on the values, qualities, and aspirations that resonate most with you. Whether you want to embody resilience, compassion, joy, or purpose, identifying this vision provides the compass for your actions.

Self-Concordant Goals: Motivation That Lasts

Psychologists describe goals as **self-concordant** when they align with your intrinsic values and authentic desires. These are the goals that feel like an extension of who you are—not dictated by societal pressures or external expectations. When goals reflect your true self, they energize and sustain you.

For example:
- If health and vitality are important to you, inspired action might mean choosing nourishing foods or engaging in movement you enjoy.

- If connection and kindness resonate, inspired action might involve reaching out to a friend or practicing forgiveness.

- If growth and creativity motivate you, inspired action might include starting a new project or exploring a passion.

Turning Vision Into Action

The bridge between aspiration and reality is intentional action. To live in alignment with who you want to be, your daily choices must reflect your values and goals.

 Try This: Aligning Actions With the RECOVERY Principles

Use this exercise to align your actions with the RECOVERY principles, promoting reflection and growth.

Step 1: Choose One Area of Focus for Each Principle Reflect on the RECOVERY principles and identify a growth area for each. Use the questions below to guide your thinking.

R: Resilience and Growth
Reflection Question: "What action can I take today to build resilience and foster growth?"
Example: "I will write down one challenge I overcame this week and what it taught me."

E: Empathy and Self-Compassion
Reflection Question: "How can I practice self-compassion in tough moments?"
Example: "When I feel frustrated, I'll pause and say, 'I'm doing the best I can.'"

C: Connection and Positive Relationships
Reflection Question: "What step can I take to nurture a relationship?"

Example: "I'll text a friend and schedule time to reconnect."

O: Optimism and Gratitude
Reflection Question: "How can I shift my focus toward gratitude?"
Example: "I'll write three things I'm grateful for before bed."

V: Vitality and Health
Reflection Question: "What choice can I make to support my physical well-being?"
Example: "I'll take a 10-minute walk or drink more water today."

E: Engagement and Purpose
Reflection Question: "What action can I take to feel more aligned with my purpose?"
Example: "I'll spend 20 minutes working on a meaningful project."

R: Reflection and Mindfulness
Reflection Question: "How can I bring more mindfulness into my routine?"
Example: "I'll practice deep breathing for 5 minutes before bed."

Y: You-Focused Empowerment
Reflection Question: "What progress can I celebrate today?"
Example: "I'll acknowledge one win, no matter how small, in my journal."

Step 2: Track and Reflect At the end of each day, journal your progress using this prompt:
Daily Reflection: "What actions did I take today? How did they make me feel?"

Step 3: Celebrate and Adjust At the end of the week, reflect on your progress with this prompt:
Weekly Reflection: "What did I learn? What worked well, and what can I improve?"

Living With Intention
Each intentional action is a step closer to the person you want to be. By consciously aligning your choices with your values, you create a life filled with purpose and meaning. Progress, not perfection, is what matters.

Celebrate every small win, and let it reinforce your belief in your ability to grow. Inspired action isn't just about what you do—it's about approaching life with clarity and intention, building momentum for meaningful, lasting transformation.

Start small. Stay consistent. And let each step guide you toward the life you're meant to live.

A Life Designed By You
When you align your actions with your values and aspirations, you create a life that feels authentic and fulfilling. Each inspired action you take brings you closer to becoming the person you want to be. Over time, this alignment transforms not only your behaviors but also your sense of identity, building a life that reflects your truest self.

Take a moment to reflect:
- What small, intentional action can you take today to align with who you want to be?

- How can you honor your vision through your choices?

Remember, inspired action is the bridge between where you are and where you want to go. Each step, no matter how small, is a testament to your growth, your resilience, and your commitment to creating a life that truly aligns with you.

Let this be your guide to becoming the person you are meant to be—one inspired action at a time.

Final Summary: Building Your Recovery Blueprint

Transformation begins with clarity, small actions, and intentional steps that align with your vision for a fulfilling life. Your recovery blueprint is a dynamic guide—a map designed to help you navigate the ups and downs of recovery while keeping your focus on what matters most. By combining self-awareness, actionable goals, and inspired action, you can move beyond fleeting motivation and build habits that reflect your values. This journey isn't about perfection; it's about progress, one deliberate step at a time.

Your RECOVERY Sunshine Assessment offers a powerful tool to revisit and refine your approach, helping you celebrate growth and identify areas for nurturing. Pairing the power of hope—where willpower meets waypower—with Minimum Viable Interventions ensures that no step is too small to create meaningful change. Through consistent, intentional actions,

> you're not just leaving old patterns behind; you're designing a life that radiates resilience, joy, and empowerment.

Three Key Takeaways

Hope Thrives on Clarity and Action
Recovery begins with the synergy of willpower and waypower. Hope grows when you pair your determination with a clear plan, ensuring every step forward is purposeful and achievable.

Small Changes Lead to Big Results
Consistent, incremental actions, such as Minimum Viable Interventions, create lasting transformation. Over time, these small steps reinforce habits, strengthen resilience, and align you with your values.

Reflection Fuels Progress
Tools like the RECOVERY Sunshine Assessment help you celebrate strengths and recalibrate areas for growth. Regular reflection keeps your recovery dynamic, ensuring your efforts remain aligned with your evolving vision.

A SPARK of HOPE

Keep Moving Toward the Light

Recovery is not a sprint; it's an unfolding—a series of small, intentional choices that together create something extraordinary. Every action you take, no matter how small, is a declaration of the life you are building. Celebrate the wins, no matter how minor they may feel. They are the threads weaving a life of purpose, joy, and fulfillment.

When setbacks arise, remember: resilience is not about avoiding challenges; it's about growing stronger in their presence. Revisit your blueprint, recalibrate, and take the next step. You are not just aiming for change—you are becoming someone new.

You have the tools, the vision, and the strength to move forward. Trust in your process, honor your progress, and keep shining. One step at a time, you are building a future that feels truly aligned and beautifully your own.

What sparked your curiosity or caught your attention?
(Reflect on what you found interesting or intriguing.)

_____
_____
_____
_____
_____

What insights or ideas feel actionable or relevant to your life?
(Identify what you can apply or implement.)

_____
_____
_____
_____
_____

What resonated deeply or felt personally meaningful to you?
(Consider what moved or inspired you emotionally or intellectually.)

_____
_____
_____
_____
_____

CHAPTER 12

Building Lasting Change—From Intentions to Habits

To bring about lasting change, we must turn good intentions into actions, and actions into habits that align with our values. True transformation isn't built overnight; it's a slow, steady unfolding that requires patience, self-compassion, and resilience. Each habit we cultivate becomes a stepping stone, creating a path toward a life filled with happiness, joy, and balance.

BUILDING HABITS THAT LAST

"The journey of a thousand miles begins with one step." — Lao Tzu

Change begins with a single step but thrives through consistency and intentionality. In this chapter, we explore how to move beyond temporary bursts of motivation to create meaningful, sustainable transformation. Lasting change isn't about perfection—it's about aligning your actions with your core values, building a life rooted in purpose and fulfillment.

Using tools like **Commitment and Declaration**, **Implementation Intentions**, and the **Elements of Change—Reminders, Rituals, Repetition, and Routines**—you'll learn how to move from aspiration to action and establish habits that support your ongoing growth.

Commitment and Declaration: Aligning with Your Values

Lasting change begins with a commitment—a deliberate decision to align your actions with the person you want to become. A personal declaration acts as a guiding force, grounding you in your values and providing clarity during moments of doubt.

Create Your Personal Commitment Declaration
Now it's your turn to craft a declaration that reflects your unique journey. This is your opportunity to articulate your intention to reclaim your life, break free from harmful patterns, and build a future aligned with your values.

Template for Your Declaration:
- **I am committed to** [describe what you are committing to—your well-being, recovery, growth, etc.].
- **I trust in my ability to** [list the strengths you believe in or want to nurture—your ability to grow, change, stay resilient, or face challenges].
- **When challenges arise, I will** [outline a positive action or mindset you will turn to in difficult moments].
- **This commitment matters because** [describe why this journey is important to you—your values, your life, or the future you envision for yourself].

Example Declaration:
"I am committed to reclaiming my life and breaking free from harmful patterns. I trust in my ability to grow, stay resilient, and make meaningful changes, even in the face of challenges. When challenges arise, I will remind myself of my strength and choose to take small, positive steps forward. This commitment matters because I deserve a life filled with well-being, joy, and purpose, and I am worthy of this transformation."

This declaration serves as a compass, reminding you of your purpose and strengthening your resolve during difficult times. Keep it visible—on your mirror, in your journal, or as a daily affirmation.

The Elements of Change: From Intention to Habit
To turn intentions into habits, you need a clear framework. The Elements of Change—Reminders, Rituals, Repetition, and Routines—work together to support lasting transformation.

Reminders: Daily Triggers for Action
Reminders act as cues that prompt you to take intentional action. Whether it's a sticky note, a phone alarm, or a habit tracker, these small signals keep your goals front and center.
Example: Set a reminder to practice gratitude each evening or place a journal by your bed to encourage nightly reflection.

Rituals: Adding Meaning to Actions
Rituals transform simple actions into meaningful practices. They provide structure and intention, turning repetitive tasks into anchors of stability.
Example: Begin your morning with a mindfulness practice or end your day by journaling three things you're grateful for.

Repetition: Strengthening Neural Pathways
Repetition is the foundation of habit formation. Each time you repeat a positive action, you reinforce neural pathways in your brain, making the behavior feel more natural over time.
Example: Commit to journaling daily for one month or take a mindful walk every afternoon.

Routines: Creating Sustainable Systems
When rituals are repeated consistently, they evolve into routines—habits that fit seamlessly into your daily life. Routines reduce reliance on willpower, making positive actions feel automatic.
Example: Incorporate a gratitude practice into your morning routine or establish a nightly wind-down routine with mindful breathing.

Implementation Intentions: Turning Plans Into Action

Motivation is fleeting, but **implementation intentions** create a roadmap for action. These "if-then" plans help you respond to challenges with clarity and purpose.

How They Work

Implementation intentions pair specific triggers ("if") with planned responses ("then"). For example:

- *If I feel overwhelmed, then I will take three deep breaths and refocus on one task.*
- *If I notice self-critical thoughts, then I will pause and replace them with a positive affirmation.*

Creating Your Plans

Identify common challenges or triggers in your life, and create clear, actionable responses for each. Write them down or rehearse them mentally to strengthen their impact.

Example Implementation Intentions:

- *If I feel tempted by old habits, then I will remind myself of my commitment and engage in a grounding activity.*
- *If I feel isolated, then I will text a trusted friend or attend a support group.*

Priming Your Environment for Success

Your environment plays a crucial role in shaping your habits. By making small adjustments to your surroundings, you can remove unnecessary triggers and create spaces that support your goals.

Steps to Prime Your Environment:
1. **Remove Negative Triggers**
   Eliminate objects or influences that remind you of harmful patterns.

2. **Introduce Positive Cues**
   Place affirmations, journals, or recovery-related tools in visible locations.

3. **Create Dedicated Spaces**
   Set up areas for mindfulness, creativity, or self-care.

4. **Build a Supportive Network**
   Surround yourself with people who encourage your growth and well-being.

Rules to Live By: Creating Personal Guidelines for Success

To create lasting change, clear and actionable guidelines—**Rules to Live By**—can help bridge the gap between intentions and habits. These personal rules align with your values and recovery goals, simplifying decisions and reinforcing your commitment to growth.

What Are Rules to Live By?
Rules to Live By are straightforward, self-imposed guidelines that reflect your priorities and support your recovery journey. These rules eliminate decision fatigue, reinforce positive behaviors, and serve as anchors in moments of uncertainty.

Examples include:
- *"I only drink wine on weekends."*
- *"I move my body for at least 10 minutes every day."*
- *"I write down three things I'm grateful for each night."*

Why They Work
Simplify Choices: Clear rules reduce the mental energy spent on decision-making.

Build Identity: Following your rules reinforces your identity as someone committed to positive change.

Foster Momentum: Consistent actions create lasting habits.

How to Create Rules to Live By
Start with Your Priorities: Use the RECOVERY principles as inspiration. For example:

If *Connection* feels dim, your rule might be: *"I reach out to one friend or family member weekly."*

If *Resilience* needs strengthening: *"I reflect on one challenge I overcame each week."*

Keep Them Simple: Choose actionable and realistic rules, like: *"I meditate for five minutes each morning."*

Write Them Down: Document your rules in a visible spot, like a journal or phone, as a daily reminder.

Examples by RECOVERY Principle
Optimism and Gratitude: *"I start each day by naming one thing I'm looking forward to."*

Vitality and Health: *"I drink a glass of water before every meal."*

Reflection and Mindfulness: *"I pause for three deep breaths whenever I feel stressed."*

Rules to Live By aren't about restriction—they're about creating freedom through clarity. By committing to these simple, values-driven guidelines, you make positive choices effortless and align your daily actions with the person you're becoming.

The "As If" Principle: Shaping Belief Through Action

Have you ever heard the phrase, "Fake it till you make it"? As discussed in the principle You-Focused Empowerment, the "As If" principle suggests that by acting as if something is already true, you can shift your mindset, emotions, and identity. This powerful tool helps you step into the life you're striving to build, even before you fully believe it's possible.

The Science Behind Acting "As If"
Psychologist Ellen Langer's 1979 study revealed that elderly participants who acted as if they were younger experienced measurable improvements in physical and mental health. This demonstrates how behavior can influence beliefs and create pro-

found change. Similarly, consistent, positive actions reinforce an identity aligned with growth and recovery.

Applying the "As If" Principle in Recovery
In recovery, acting as if you're already living a life aligned with your goals can create a self-fulfilling prophecy. When you embody your aspirations, you internalize those behaviors over time.

Physical Actions: Walk confidently, engage in routines that align with well-being, and prioritize purposeful activities.

Empowering Language: Speak in ways that affirm your growth, like, "I am someone who chooses peace and balance."

Aligned Decisions: Make choices that reflect the person you're becoming, even in small moments.

This practice isn't about ignoring challenges—it's about intentionally choosing actions that align with your future self.

How It Works: Behavior, Belief, Identity
The principle leverages a cycle of growth:

- **Behavior Shapes Belief**: Actions convince your mind that change is real.

- **Belief Shapes Identity**: New beliefs foster confidence in your ability to grow.

- **Identity Shapes Behavior**: Positive behaviors become second nature, reinforcing the cycle.

Steps to Act "As If"
1. **Visualize Your Ideal Life**: Imagine how the best version of yourself thinks, feels, and acts.

2. **Start Small**: Choose one behavior that reflects this vision.

3. **Adopt Empowering Language**: Speak as though progress has already been made.

4. **Create Positive Cues**: Use affirmations, vision boards, or reminders to keep goals top of mind.

5. **Celebrate Progress**: Acknowledge each step, reinforcing your belief in growth.

Building the Life You Want
The "As If" principle shifts focus from what you're leaving behind to what you're building. By acting as if you're already the person you aspire to be, you create new neural pathways that make positive behaviors easier and more natural over time.

Start today with one small act: adopt a confident posture, make a nourishing choice, or reach out for connection. Each step reinforces your belief in your ability to transform.

Summary

This chapter explored the art of transforming good intentions into sustainable habits. True change emerges through small, consistent steps that align with your values and aspirations.

By embracing tools like personal commitment declarations, the Elements of Change, implementation intentions, rules to live by, and the "As If" principle, you can navigate the complexities of recovery and personal growth with clarity and purpose.

These strategies create a comprehensive framework for aligning your daily actions with your long-term vision, helping you build a life filled with resilience, balance, and joy. Each element reinforces the others, turning fleeting motivation into lasting transformation.

Three Key Takeaways

Intentionality Fuels Transformation
Real change begins with commitment and intentionality. A personal declaration serves as a compass, grounding you in your values and guiding your actions during challenging moments.

Small Steps Create Lasting Habits
The Elements of Change—Reminders, Rituals, Repetition, and Routines—form the foundation of habit formation. These small, deliberate actions build momentum, making positive behaviors effortless over time.

Act as If You've Already Changed
The "As If" principle empowers you to embody the person you aspire to be, creating a self-reinforcing cycle of belief, identity, and action. By behaving as though transformation is already underway, you pave the way for lasting growth.

A SPARK of HOPE

Your Journey Forward

This book has been your guide to reclaiming your life and creating a future rooted in meaning, resilience, and joy. By weaving together the RECOVERY principles, actionable tools, and mindset shifts, you've explored not only how to overcome harmful patterns but also how to design a life that aligns with your deepest values.

Through self-awareness, intentional action, and the support of practical frameworks, you've gained the clarity and confidence to navigate your unique journey. Recovery is not about perfection—it's about progress, self-compassion, and the courage to start again, one step at a time.

Your recovery is more than just a process—it's a testament to your strength, resilience, and commitment to growth. The tools and principles in this book are now yours to adapt and apply, guiding you through challenges and celebrating your triumphs.

Remember, transformation is not about achieving an end state but embracing the ongoing process of becoming. Each small step forward, each intentional action, reinforces your belief in your capacity to grow. You are not defined by your past but by the choices you make today and the life you're building for tomorrow.

Take a moment to reflect: What will your next step be? Whether it's writing a final commitment letter to your future self, setting a new goal, or reaching out for connection, each action reinforces your path toward lasting recovery and well-being.

This is your time to shine. Keep going, keep growing, and trust in your ability to create the life you deserve. You've got this!

What sparked your curiosity or caught your attention?
(Reflect on what you found interesting or intriguing.)

_____
_____
_____
_____

What insights or ideas feel actionable or relevant to your life?
(Identify what you can apply or implement.)

_____
_____
_____
_____

What resonated deeply or felt personally meaningful to you?
(Consider what moved or inspired you emotionally or intellectually.)

_____
_____
_____
_____

Conclusion

A Final Wish for You

Dear Reader,

As you close these pages, I want to take a moment to speak directly to your heart. This journey of recovery you're on is nothing short of heroic. It is a path that not only leads you away from old, addictive behaviors but, more importantly, toward reclaiming the person you truly are. This isn't just about overcoming behaviors that no longer serve you—it's about rediscovering the vast potential that has always lived within you.

I want you to know that you are never alone. Even in moments when you feel isolated, love and support are all around you as you recover. Friends, family, and even those you may not realize are cheering you on, lifting you up. They see you, not defined by your struggle, but as a person of immense strength, possibility, and grace.

My deepest wish for you is a life filled with joy, peace, and fulfillment. I wish for you to wake each morning with a sense of purpose, knowing that every day is a new opportunity to create a life that reflects your inner strength and beauty. May you walk with resilience in the face of adversity, finding compassion for yourself in moments of challenge. And when the journey feels steep, may you discover the courage to keep moving forward, knowing that you are always moving closer to your freedom.

I wish for you to build relationships that nourish your soul, connections that lift you up and remind you of your infinite worth. Surround yourself with people who see the light in you and reflect it back when you need it most. These relationships will be your steady anchor, a source of love and encouragement as you grow and thrive.

May you find beauty in the small, simple moments, and may you never lose sight of the goodness that exists both in the world and within you. Celebrate your victories, no matter how small they seem, and let gratitude be the force that carries you forward.

Remember, recovery is not a destination but a lifelong journey of rediscovery. Be gentle with yourself, for you are human, and setbacks do not define you—they are simply part of the unfolding story of your strength and wisdom.

Take the lessons and principles of this book with you as companions on your path. Let them serve as reminders of the incredible power you hold to shape your own life, to create a future filled with love, possibility, and freedom.

My deepest wish is for you to live a life where you can flourish, where you are free from the grip of addictive behaviors and connected to the person you were always meant to be. You are worthy of all the joy, all the peace, and all the abundance that life has to offer. I believe in you completely.

With love and unwavering support,

Andrea Seydel

CONCLUSION

P.S. As you continue your journey, I invite you to stay connected. Visit our website for resources, monthly meetings, and opportunities. You are not alone—our community is here to support you every step of the way.

www.readyforrecovery.life

Share Your Journey and Inspire Others

Has the *Recovery Without Rock Bottom* podcast or the *Ready for Recovery* community made an impact on your life? If this book has helped you on your journey, we'd love to hear from you! Your experiences and insights can inspire others to discover the power of recovery and transformation.

Write a Review
Share your thoughts about this book by leaving a review on Amazon or wherever you purchased it. Your review not only helps others find this resource but also spreads hope and encouragement to those seeking change.

Submit a Testimonial
Visit **ReadyForRecovery.life** to submit a testimonial about how this book, our podcast, or community has impacted your life. Whether you prefer a written message or a video, your story is valuable and deeply appreciated. Together, we can shine a light on the path to resilience, strength, and empowerment.

Be a Guest or Get Featured
We're always looking for stories of hope, strength, and resilience to feature on the *Recovery Without Rock Bottom* podcast and in the *Ready for Recovery* magazine. Share your journey, and you could inspire countless others as a guest on our podcast or as a featured story in our magazine.

Spread the Ripple Effect of Positivity
Your participation helps create a ripple effect of positivity and happiness that touches countless lives. By sharing your experiences, you're contributing to a growing community of individuals committed to transformation, resilience, and purpose.

Take Action Today
- Leave a review online.
- Submit your testimonial at www.**ReadyForRecovery.life**.
- Share this book with friends, loved ones, or professionals in your network.
- Become part of the movement by being a guest on our podcast or featured in our magazine.

Your story matters, and your voice has the power to inspire change. Thank you for being part of this journey. Together, we are building a stronger, more hopeful world.

Ready for Recovery

Welcome to *Ready for Recovery*—your companion on the path to growth, healing, and transformation. By reading this book, you've already set powerful intentions for growth and transformation. Now, it's time to build on that momentum and deepen your journey with *Ready for Recovery*. Together, we can create a ripple effect of resilience, hope, and happiness that transforms not only your life but the lives of those around you.. This book is your gateway to a vibrant community, expert resources, and practical tools that empower individuals and professionals alike to thrive.

How to Get Involved
Your journey continues with *Ready for Recovery*:

- **Monthly Community Meetings**: Join our uplifting online gatherings for connection, sharing, and support.

- **Magazine & Training Center**: Explore the *Ready for Recovery* magazine for expert advice, inspiring stories, and actionable insights. Dive deeper with training programs designed for individuals and professionals.

- **Podcast: Recovery Without Rock Bottom**: Tune in to inspiring episodes that provide guidance, tools, and stories of hope from those who've walked the path.

- **Recovery Coach Certification & Training**: Become a certified Recovery Coach using the RECOVERY principles.

Perfect for individuals and professionals seeking a high-impact way to make a difference.

For Professionals: Train the Trainer
Are you a psychologist, psychotherapist, doctor, social worker, treatment center owner, or group facilitator? Incorporate *Recovery Without Rock Bottom* into your practice or treatment center to enhance success rates:

- **High Success Rate Recovery Coach Certification**: Train the trainer to empower your staff with our proven methods.
- **Customizable Kits & Bulk Orders**: Equip your clients and teams with tailored resources at discounted rates.
- **Practical Tools**: Access the *Recovery Sunshine Assessment* and other transformative exercises to inspire lasting change.

Our Mission
At *Ready for Recovery,* we are redefining what it means to recover. Recovery is not just about breaking free from harmful behaviors—it's about reclaiming your potential, rediscovering joy, and building a purposeful, empowered life. Our mission is to destigmatize recovery and celebrate the strength and resilience it takes to grow through life's challenges.

We believe in the ripple effect of positivity and happiness. Every action we take, every story we share, and every life we touch creates waves of healing and empowerment. Together, we aim to spread resilience, connection, and hope to individuals, families, and communities around the world.

Join the Ripple Effect
You can help create a brighter future:

- **Spread the Word**: Share this book, recommend it to colleagues, and introduce others to our community.
- **Give the Gift of Recovery**: Purchase copies for loved ones, clients, or organizations in need.
- **Support Our Mission**: Every donation goes toward expanding our platform, creating conversation kits, and providing resources to underserved communities.

Take Your Next Step Forward
Visit ReadyForRecovery.life to:

Access the *Recovery Sunshine Assessment* and other exclusive tools (scan the QR code to get started).

Learn about upcoming community events, training programs, and certification opportunities.

Discover how you can be part of the ripple effect, spreading positivity and purpose in your community.

Together, let's build a world where recovery is a journey of empowerment and joy, inspiring positive change that touches countless lives.

About the Author

Andrea Seydel is a passionate advocate for personal growth, well-being, and resilience. With a Master's degree in Happiness Studies and postgraduate education in Positive Psychology, Andrea is also a Certified Positive Psychology Coach, bringing science-based strategies to help individuals and communities thrive.

Andrea is the author of the empowering book series *Saving You is Killing Me: Loving Someone with an Addiction*, which has inspired countless readers to reclaim their lives and find strength in challenging circumstances. Her expertise and compassion shine through her writing, speaking, and coaching, empowering others to overcome adversity and embrace happiness.

Andrea is also the creator of the *Ready for Recovery* community, which includes the *Recovery Without Rock Bottom* podcast, the *Ready for Recovery* magazine, and the Recovery Coach Certification program, providing accessible tools and training for professionals and individuals alike.

When she's not writing or coaching, Andrea is a proud mom to four children and two golden retrievers. Recently married, she's enjoying life's adventures with her husband, whether it's hiking scenic trails, playing outdoors, or traveling to explore new destinations. At home, Andrea finds joy in her feathered companion, Birdmango, who keeps life entertaining.

Through her work, Andrea's mission is to create a ripple effect of positivity and well-being, empowering others to build a life filled with purpose, joy, and resilience. www.andreaseydel.com

References

Achor, S. (2010). *The happiness advantage: How a positive brain fuels success in work and life.* Crown Business.

Baer, R. A. (2003). Mindfulness training as a clinical intervention: A conceptual and empirical review. *Clinical Psychology: Science and Practice, 10*(2), 125–143.

Bandura, A. (1977). Self-efficacy: Toward a unifying theory of behavioral change. *Psychological Review, 84*(2), 191–215.

Bandura, A. (1997). *Self-efficacy: The exercise of control.* W.H. Freeman.

Baumeister, R. F., & Tierney, J. (2011). *Willpower: Rediscovering the greatest human strength.* Penguin Press.

Beck, A. T. (1976). *Cognitive therapy and the emotional disorders.* International Universities Press.

Ben-Shahar, T. (2007). *Happier: Learn the secrets to daily joy and lasting fulfillment.* McGraw-Hill.

Ben-Shahar, T. (2009). *Even happier: A gratitude journal for daily joy and lasting fulfillment.* McGraw-Hill.

Ben-Shahar, T. (2009). *The pursuit of perfect: How to stop chasing perfection and start living a richer, happier life.* McGraw-Hill.

Ben-Shahar, T. (2012). *Choose the life you want: 101 ways to create your own road to happiness.* The Experiment.

Ben-Shahar, T., & Ridgway, A. (2017). *The joy of leadership: How positive psychology can maximize your impact (and make you happier) in a challenging world.* Wiley.

Ben-Shahar, T. (2021). *Happier, no matter what: Cultivating hope, resilience, and purpose in hard times.* The Experiment.

Brown, B. (2015). *Rising strong: The reckoning, the rumble, the revolution.* Spiegel & Grau.

Brown, K. W., & Ryan, R. M. (2003). The benefits of being present: Mindfulness and its role in psychological well-being. *Journal of Personality and Social Psychology, 84*(4), 822–848.

Carter, C. S. (2014). Oxytocin pathways and the evolution of human behavior. Annual Review of Psychology, 65, 17–39.

Carver, C. S., Scheier, M. F., & Segerstrom, S. C. (2010). Optimism. Clinical Psychology Review, 30(7), 879–889.

Clear, J. (2018). Atomic habits: An easy & proven way to build good habits & break bad ones. Avery.

Cohen, S., & Wills, T. A. (1985). Stress, social support, and the buffering hypothesis. Psychological Bulletin, 98(2), 310–357.

Csikszentmihalyi, M. (1990). Flow: The psychology of optimal experience. Harper & Row.

Deci, E. L., & Ryan, R. M. (1985). Intrinsic motivation and self-determination in human behavior. Springer Science & Business Media.

Duhigg, C. (2012). The power of habit: Why we do what we do in life and business. Random House.

Dweck, C. S. (2006). Mindset: The new psychology of success. Random House.

Emmons, R. A., & McCullough, M. E. (2003). Counting blessings versus burdens: An experimental investigation of gratitude and subjective well-being in daily life. Journal of Personality and Social Psychology, 84(2), 377–389.

Fredrickson, B. L. (2001). The role of positive emotions in positive psychology: The broaden-and-build theory of positive emotions. American Psychologist, 56(3), 218–226.

Fredrickson, B. L. (2004). The broaden-and-build theory of positive emotions. Philosophical Transactions of the Royal Society B: Biological Sciences, 359(1449), 1367–1377.

Fredrickson, B. L. (2009). Positivity: Top-notch research reveals the 3-to-1 ratio that will change your life. Crown Publishing Group.

Frankl, V. E. (2006). Man's search for meaning. Beacon Press.

Gable, S. L., Reis, H. T., Impett, E. A., & Asher, E. R. (2004). What do you do when things go right? The intrapersonal and interpersonal benefits of sharing positive events. Journal of Personality and Social Psychology, 87(2), 228–245.

Germer, C. K., & Neff, K. D. (2013). Self-compassion in clinical practice. Journal of Clinical Psychology, 69(8), 856–867.

Gilbert, D. (2006). Stumbling on happiness. Vintage.

Gollwitzer, P. M. (1999). Implementation intentions: Strong effects of simple plans. American Psychologist, 54(7), 493–503.

Gross, J. J. (2002). Emotion regulation: Affective, cognitive, and social consequences. Psychophysiology, 39(3), 281–291.

Harris, R. (2008). The happiness trap: How to stop struggling and start living. Shambhala.

Hayes, S. C., Strosahl, K. D., & Wilson, K. G. (1999). Acceptance and commitment therapy: An experiential approach to behavior change. Guilford Press.

Hayes, S. C., Strosahl, K. D., & Wilson, K. G. (2011). Acceptance and commitment therapy: The process and practice of mindful change (2nd ed.). Guilford Press.

Hölzel, B. K., Carmody, J., Vangel, M., Congleton, C., Yerramsetti, S. M., Gard, T., & Lazar, S. W. (2011). Mindfulness practice leads to increases in regional brain gray matter density. Psychiatry Research: Neuroimaging, 191(1), 36–43.

Hyman, M. (2018). Food: What the heck should I eat? Little, Brown Spark.

Kabat-Zinn, J. (1990). Full catastrophe living: Using the wisdom of your body and mind to face stress, pain, and illness. Delta.

Kabat-Zinn, J. (2005). Wherever you go, there you are: Mindfulness meditation in everyday life. Hachette Books.

King, L. A. (2001). The health benefits of writing about life goals. Personality and Social Psychology Bulletin, 27(7), 798–807.

Lieberman, M. D. (2013). Social: Why our brains are wired to connect. Crown Publishing Group.

Loehr, J., & Schwartz, T. (2003). The power of full engagement: Managing energy, not time, is the key to high performance and personal renewal. Free Press.

Mandela, N. (1994). Long walk to freedom: The autobiography of Nelson Mandela. Little, Brown.

Neff, K. D. (2003). *Self-compassion: An alternative conceptualization of a healthy attitude toward oneself. Self and Identity, 2(2),* 85–101.

Neff, K. D. (2011). *Self-compassion: The proven power of being kind to yourself.* HarperCollins.

Neff, K. D., & Germer, C. K. (2018). *The mindful self-compassion workbook: A proven way to accept yourself, build inner strength, and thrive.* Guilford Press.

Oettingen, G. (2014). *Rethinking positive thinking: Inside the new science of motivation.* Current.

Pennebaker, J. W. (1997). *Writing about emotional experiences as a therapeutic process. Psychological Science, 8(3),* 162–166.

Peterson, C., & Seligman, M. E. P. (2004). *Character strengths and virtues: A handbook and classification.* Oxford University Press.

Prochaska, J. O., Norcross, J. C., & DiClemente, C. C. (1994). *Changing for good: A revolutionary six-stage program for overcoming bad habits and moving your life positively forward.* William Morrow.

Ratey, J. J. (2008). *Spark: The revolutionary new science of exercise and the brain.* Little, Brown and Company.

Ryff, C. D., & Keyes, C. L. M. (1995). *The structure of psychological well-being revisited. Journal of Personality and Social Psychology, 69(4),* 719–727.

Sarris, J., Logan, A. C., & Akbaraly, T. N. (2015). *Nutritional medicine as mainstream in psychiatry. The Lancet Psychiatry, 2(3),* 271–274.

Schein, E. H. (2013). *Humble inquiry: The gentle art of asking instead of telling.* Berrett-Koehler Publishers.

Seligman, M. E. P. (1991). *Learned optimism: How to change your mind and your life.* Vintage.

Seligman, M. E. P. (2002). *Authentic happiness: Using the new positive psychology to realize your potential for lasting fulfillment.* Free Press.

Seligman, M. E. P. (2011). *Flourish: A visionary new understanding of happiness and well-being.* Atria Books.

Siegel, D. J. (2012). *The developing mind: How relationships and the brain interact to shape who we are.* Guilford Press.

Tomasulo, D. J. (2020). Learned hopefulness: The power of positivity to overcome depression. New World Library.

Van der Kolk, B. A. (2014). The body keeps the score: Brain, mind, and body in the healing of trauma. Viking.

Volkow, N. D., Koob, G. F., & McLellan, A. T. (2016). Neurobiologic advances from the brain disease model of addiction. New England Journal of Medicine, 374(4), 363–371.

Walker, M. P. (2017). Why we sleep: Unlocking the power of sleep and dreams. Scribner.

Wood, A. M., Froh, J. J., & Geraghty, A. W. A. (2010). Gratitude and well-being: A review and theoretical integration. Clinical Psychology Review, 30(7), 890–905.

About The Publisher

Dear Reader,

As you hold this remarkable book in your hands, we want to express our heartfelt gratitude for becoming a part of the Live Life Happy Community of readers. Your curiosity and thirst for knowledge fuel our passion for publishing meaningful non-fiction works.

At Live Life Happy Publishing, our mission is rooted in bringing forth literature that not only entertains but uplifts, supports, and nourishes the soul. We firmly believe that books have the power to transform lives, to ignite passions, and to spread joy far and wide.

Behind every word, every chapter, lies the dedication of our authors who pour their hearts and souls into their craft. Their ultimate aim? To touch your life in profound ways, to inspire, and to leave an indelible mark on your journey.

Your role in this journey is invaluable; by sharing your thoughts through reviews, spreading the word to others, or reaching out to the authors themselves, you become an integral part of sparking transformation in countless lives, igniting a ripple effect of joy and enlightenment.

And if, perchance, you or someone you know has dreams of writing, of sharing a message, or of unleashing a powerful story unto the world, know that Live Life Happy Publishing stands ready to guide you. Our doors are open, our ears attuned, and our hearts eager to hear your message.

So, dear reader, let us, continue to spread the power of literature, one page at a time. Reach out, share, and most importantly, never underestimate the power of your message to touch lives.

With warmest regards,

LiveLifeHappyPublishing.com

P.S. Remember, books change lives. Whose life will you touch with yours?

www.ingramcontent.com/pod-product-compliance
Lightning Source LLC
Chambersburg PA
CBHW060450170426
43199CB00011B/1150